GW00372668

Chair Anatomy

Design and Construction

James Orrom

With over 700 illustrations

T&H

Contents

First published in the United Kingdom
in 2018 by Thames & Hudson Ltd,
181A High Holborn, London WC1V 7QX

First paperback edition 2020

Chair Anatomy: Design and Construction
© 2018 Thames & Hudson Ltd, London

Text © 2018 James Orrom
Photographs © 2018 James Orrom,
unless otherwise stated on p. 240
Line drawings © 2018 Victoria Orrom

Designed by Samuel Clark
www.bytheskydesign.com

British Library Cataloguing-in-
Publication Data
A catalogue record for this book is
available from the British Library

ISBN 978-0-500-29594-6

Printed in China by RR Donnelley

To find out about all our publications,
please visit **www.thamesandhudson**.
com. There you can subscribe to our
e-newsletter, browse or download our
current catalogue, and buy any titles that
are in print.

Introduction

This book provides young designers, collectors and design enthusiasts with a reference work about chairs. Through photos and illustrations, it reveals the form and the construction details – the *anatomy* – of more than 50 chairs from the last 150 years of modern chair design. It also introduces the designers behind these chairs, their backgrounds and their routes to creating their designs. It is not intended as an instruction manual or a how-to-do-it book for designers; nor is it intended to steer young creatives towards using standard solutions. Rather, by showing in detail the way in which materials and constructional details have been used, the book aims to provide the reader with a platform of knowledge to help them understand the methods and ideas that lie behind the designs.

Many people have a limited experience of iconic chairs. Either their visual repertoire has not had time to develop, or they have not yet been able to study seating hands-on. Inevitably, the scarcity, or value, of many well-known chairs, whether presented in a museum, exhibition setting or even a high-quality showroom, often prevents them from being touched, judged and sat on, let alone dismantled, weighed and measured.

This book thus supplies young designers with the technical information that is so often hard to obtain – right down to the smallest screw – and presents it in a highly visual form. It offers them the chance to learn about specific design details in a manner previously unavailable, and to see elements of the selected chairs in unprecedented clarity. To understand that a particular aesthetically pleasing solution is based on a specific construction is not only satisfying but also can be the vital step towards realizing new ideas and solutions.

A common error in many preliminary chair-design experiments, whether in college or a design practice, is the oversizing of materials. Out of an uncertainty about the mechanical properties of the chosen materials, the dimensions are often exaggerated, just to be on the safe side. This book shows how similar problems have been solved in the past, and, with respect to the featured chairs, provides the answers to the following questions: Which leg cross sections were used in which materials, and which diameter of rod, tube or extrusion?

How were the legs fixed to the seat, the backrest to the legs, and which angles were appropriate? Which production process was used? Was the chair welded, moulded, carved, cast or machined? How much did the completed chair weigh? Which finish was used, which screw size and which combination of materials? In the case of the more complex chairs, such as those with intricate joints, additional close-up photos or line drawings are used to improve understanding. In this way, the reader can get to know the chairs, recognize the design principles involved, grasp how they were put together, learn the materials employed and understand which manufacturing techniques were used in their production.

'Milestone' chairs are nearly always those that were inspired by a new material or designed using the possibilities offered by a new manufacturing technique. When it came to selecting the chairs featured in this book, it was decided that, of the myriad produced in the last 150 years, each should meet one or both of the following criteria: 1) at the time, the materials, construction methods or manufacturing processes involved were new to the field of chair design; 2) also at the time, the design concept used a radically different approach, applying a new combination of techniques. The resulting shortlist of chairs was therefore composed of those that represented an innovative decision, a definitive step – a leap forward even – in the developing history of chair design. A certain amount of personal preference was used to whittle the list down to the final 54, and it is hoped that any glaring omissions will be forgiven.

At the end of the book – together with a glossary of technical terms and a bibliography for further reading – is a section on the designers behind the selected chairs. The word 'designer' is used here in a generic way, and includes architects, industrial designers, designer-makers and even a philosopher who moved into furniture making. In an increasingly design-aware society, the designer's name is often more important than that of the manufacturer; indeed, in some cases, the designer gains celebrity status through their work. And yet all of these 'names' had to begin somewhere; all of them had to learn their trade, as must every generation that follows them. The tools (both mechanical and digital) of visualization, communication and realization may have evolved, but the creative process – blending technical knowledge with cultural and historical experience to create new forms and visual solutions – continues unchanged.

Each of these designers' backgrounds plays (or played) a large role in their design practice and, to an extent, in the origination of their furniture. In order to help the reader understand their individual approaches, each is provided with a short biography, concentrating on the formative years of their life – what and where they studied, their first job, when they started their own office, etc. In outlining the various, sometimes indirect routes

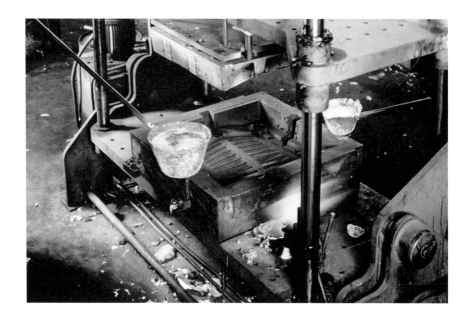

by which they began their careers, the aim is to demystify some of the aura surrounding the well-known names, and to inspire younger designers to find their own way.

Among other things, the designers come from a wide variety of backgrounds. Some are famous in their own right as architects, and produced their chairs as part of a larger building project. Others achieved a breakthrough soon after beginning their career.

Through their interest in new processes and materials, they all managed to create a landmark design, influencing other designers for years to come. By bringing together this biographical information about a core of well-known designers, it is possible to form some tentative comparisons and to identify some common denominators. That is not to say that there is a recipe for success to be found here, but it is certainly interesting to note that the majority of the featured designers actively sought out public recognition, whether in exhibitions or competitions, at an early stage in their careers, and that most of them founded their own office or practice within the first few years of completing their education. This book is intended to provide support in two important ways: as a basic technical guide to the standard canon of modern chairs, and as a reminder of the many possibilities open to young design professionals on their way to success.

A book of this kind can only ever offer an introduction to a given subject, and it is hoped that *Chair Anatomy* will not only awaken an interest in the work of a wealth of chair designers, but also – perhaps with the help of the books listed in the bibliography – encourage further personal research. Above all, the book provides a solid grounding in chair design, and a basic repertoire of information to help and inform.

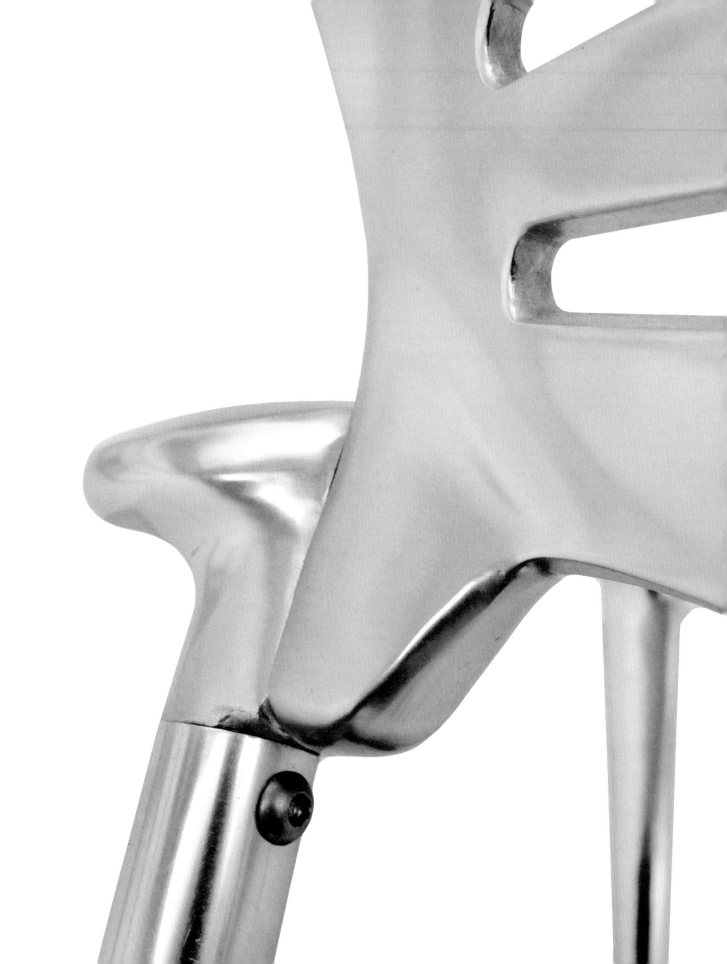

.03

Maarten Van Severen 1998

Initially, Vitra wanted to call this chair CN° III – in reference to Van Severen's 1992 chair CN° II – but that name was already being used by Thonet. The chair itself is an adaptation of CN° II (later renamed .02 by Vitra), for which Van Severen used a single layer of fine plywood as a seating surface.

The different treatment of the front and back legs is reminiscent of Jean Prouvé's Standard chair (p. 172), where the back legs are engineered to take higher loading and bending forces (from tipping and rocking) than the front. Here, the rear steel tubes are stiffer and stronger than the aluminium section at the front.

The .03 is remarkable for its apparent simplicity and secrecy: at first glance, it reveals nothing about its construction to the user. In fact, it is a complex, high-tech product – developed using the latest technology of its time – being one of the first chairs to utilize a polyurethane moulding around a welded steel frame, completely enclosing the construction.

The first surprise for the user is the flexible backrest. This is achieved by means of three spring-steel strips, similar to a leaf-spring suspension, which supply the necessary stiffness and flexibility.

The chair is also available in a stacking version, in which the back legs are set on the outside edge of the seat, as well as various office versions with a central base on castors.

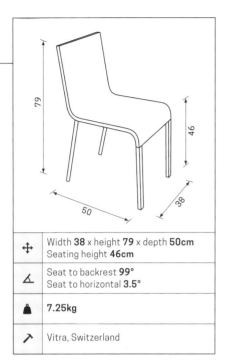

✛	Width **38** x height **79** x depth **50cm** Seating height **46cm**
◿	Seat to backrest **99°** Seat to horizontal **3.5°**
⬙	**7.25kg**
➚	Vitra, Switzerland

Construction

Seat and backrest Self-skinning polyurethane foam, WT 20mm, backrest tapering from 20mm at centre to 17.5mm at top edge. Curve at the front of seat/leg and seat/backrest R65mm.

Seat frame Sides: rectangular-section steel rod 10x20mm, extending 65mm into top of front legs, glued with epoxy visible only with an endoscope (see photos this page, first column, second and third from top). Front: rolled 1.3mm sheet steel, radius 55mm, back edge with a closed hem, front edge 90° fold.

Backrest frame Two horizontal steel strips 30x4mm, two vertical groups of three spring-steel strips 20x2mm held in 25x10mm rectangular steel section, WT 2mm. Rear corner: 15x25mm steel section holding Ø16mm rod, which extends 23mm into rear leg, internally threaded for socket-head screw to fix rear legs from inside (see photo this page, second column, second from top). Corner triangulation Ø8mm steel rod.

Front legs Rectangular aluminium extrusion, 20x30mm, WT 5mm.

Rear legs Steel seamed tube Ø20mm, WT 2mm.

Feet Grey polypropylene, 3mm visible, 25mm hidden in legs.

Surface treatment Self-coloured polyurethane, legs powder-coated semi-gloss.

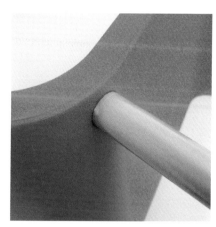
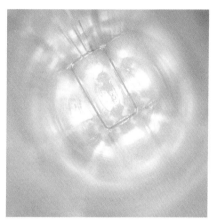

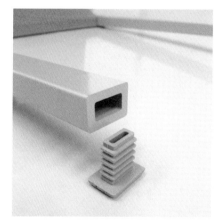

3107

Arne Jacobsen 1955

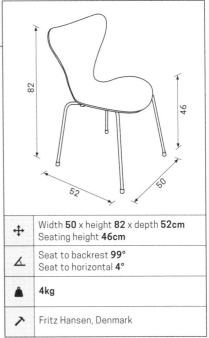

✛	Width **50** x height **82** x depth **52cm** Seating height **46cm**
⊿	Seat to backrest **99°** Seat to horizontal **4°**
⚖	**4kg**
↗	Fritz Hansen, Denmark

The 3107, one of the first commercially available chairs to use a one-piece, three-dimensionally curved plywood shell for the seat and backrest, is a further development of Jacobsen's three-legged Ant chair from 1951. By reducing the width of the bridge between seat and back, and thus the degree of bent surface, Jacobsen avoided the problems that beset the Eameses a decade before, when they were experimenting with three-dimensionally formed plywood shells: the veneer layers can be bent relatively easily in two dimensions, but tend to split when formed into compound curves. The flexibility of Jacobsen's bridge, combined with the rubber stoppers under the seat (see p. 18), provide an unexpected degree of backrest movement; they also contribute to the surprising comfort of an apparently simple chair.

The 3107 is now available in three different seating heights: 43cm, 46cm and 48cm. The line drawing above is of the 46cm version.

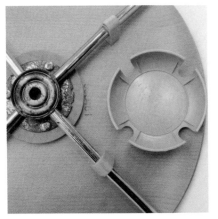

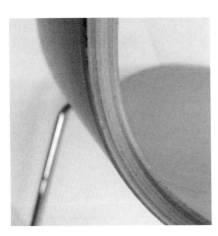

Construction

Seat and backrest Seven-layer veneered plywood, WT9.3mm. Shoulder width 50cm, bridge or 'waist' 22cm wide. Central disc of 9mm plywood for attaching legs is glued into a 1.5mm recession, to compensate for the curvature. Its outside face is Ø120mm, the inside face is turned to Ø114mm, leaving a 3mm deep, 5mm high undercut to hold the thickened edge of the bowl-shaped plastic cover (WT1.5mm with 1.5mm half-round rim on inside edge to grip plywood disc). Earlier models used a sheet-metal cover held by small metal pins (see photo this page, first column, second from bottom) instead of the plastic. The plywood disc holds three threaded M6 inserts, not equidistant, to locate the legs (which are not symmetrical). The flanges on the bottom end of the inserts (not visible) are sandwiched between seat and disc, increasing their stability.

Legs Chrome-plated steel tube Ø14mm, WT2mm; front legs 45cm apart at foot, rear legs 49.5cm. The four legs are spot-welded to two metal plates, top mounting plate Ø90mm, WT2mm, drilled 8.5mm for M6 x 14mm fillister-head slotted screws. Lower plate Ø62mm, WT2mm, blackened steel.

Four rubber stoppers (see photo this page, second column, second from bottom) regulate the flexing of the shell on the legs and prevent damage when stacking the chairs. Dimensions: 18x30mm base tapering to 9mm radius around leg, 33mm high, WT3mm. In earlier versions the stoppers were solid rubber.

Feet Two-part black nylon, inside stopper Ø14mm with 3mm rim, 13mm high, outside cap tapering from Ø18 to Ø20mm, 19mm high with 2mm dome on base, both hollow with WT2mm.

Air

Jasper Morrison 2003

The Air collection of furniture was one of the first to make use of the relatively new technique of gas-assisted moulding (also known as air-moulding), which enables the production of lighter, stronger structures. Drawing on his interest in archetypal shapes, Morrison used this new process to create a series of elegant pieces that have been reduced to the most basic form necessary, the air-moulding allowing him to dispense with visible joints and multiple parts. The collection includes a small table and four chairs: a standard stacking side chair, an armchair, and folding chairs with and without arms; illustrated here is the folding version with arms. Morrison's design refers to the classic garden chair with a slatted wooden seat, reinterpreted in the soft, tubular aesthetic of air-moulding.

During the moulding process, high-pressure gas (nitrogen) forces the molten injected plastic on to the sides of the mould, forming a tunnel or tube – a shape that is typically both stiff and light. The designs have to be carefully developed to allow the plastic and gas to flow freely through the mould.

The chair is made principally from polypropylene mixed or 'filled' with finely chopped glass fibres. However, as the fibres give the polypropylene a matt, whitish speckled surface, the mould is filled in two stages. First, a layer of pure polypropylene (bright colour, good surface quality) is injected into the mould. This is followed immediately by the fibreglass-filled polypropylene, which provides the chair with additional strength and resilience. The photo on p. 22, bottom left, shows a cross section of a similar, green air-moulded leg, clearly revealing the two-layered structure.

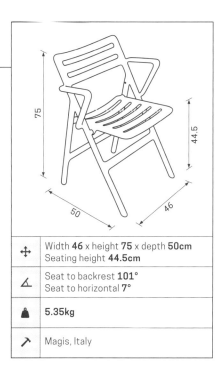

✥	Width **46** x height **75** x depth **50cm** Seating height **44.5cm**
∠	Seat to backrest **101°** Seat to horizontal **7°**
⚖	**5.35kg**
↗	Magis, Italy

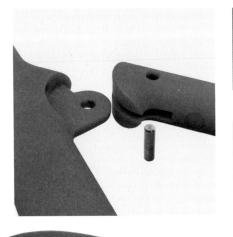

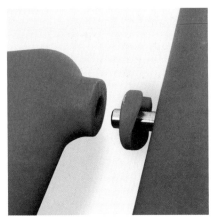

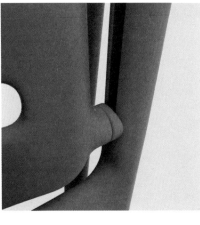

Construction

Seat, arms, backrest and legs

Polypropylene partly reinforced with fibreglass.

Legs Rounded-oval section 34x28mm at main joint, tapering to 31.5x28mm at foot. Top of back legs rounded R42mm, Ø8mm blind hole open towards inside. Leg hinged with two Ø8mm x 22mm stainless-steel rods introduced from the inside, i.e. from the middle of the chair outwards into blind hole. Hinge centre-tab on main frame 6.6mm wide, socket concave with R42mm.

Seat Pivots on Ø8mm x 30mm stainless-steel rods located in front legs. Again, the rods are introduced from inside face of seat tab into blind hole in leg. This means that the chair cannot be demounted without drilling additional holes to push out the rods from the outside.

Rear fixing of seat is also an Ø8mm x 30mm stainless-steel rod, which runs in an 8x195mm slot in the back leg, passing through a Ø24mm x 7.8mm washer. A small rectangular peg on the washer 5.7x6.7mm prevents it from turning, as does the concave R40mm surface that slides on the side surface of the leg.

Front stretcher 42x22.5mm, rear stretcher 42x23mm. Seating slats 49x15mm, slots in between 21mm.

Arms 40x18mm.

Backrest Three slats, top 40.5x24.8mm, lower two 39x16mm, slots in beteween 23mm.

Feet Clear polypropylene stopper Ø14mm x 3mm top, Ø8mm x 17mm hollow shaft WT2mm, pressed into Ø8mm hole rebated with Ø14mm x 2mm.

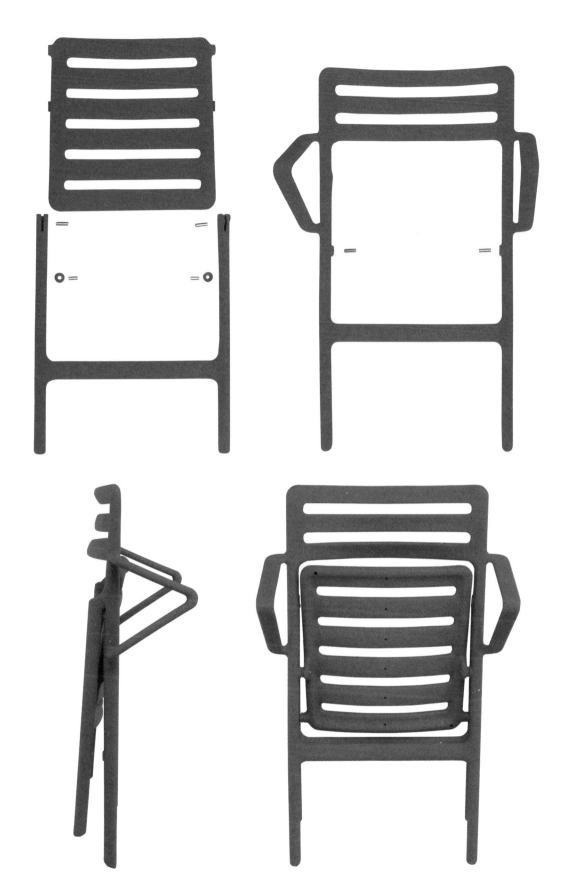

Antelope

Ernest Race 1950

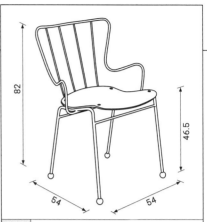

✛	Width **54** x height **82** x depth **54cm** Seating height **46.5cm**
◁	Seat to backrest **104°** Seat to horizontal **12°**
⬥	**5.95kg**
⬈	Race Furniture, UK

While Hans Coray's 1938 Landi exhibition chair (see p. 98) was an expression of Swiss national pride, the Antelope, the other exhibition chair in this book, can be seen as an exercise in British optimism. It was commisioned by the UK government to furnish the outdoor terraces of the 1951 Festival of Britain, a trade fair intended to raise public morale after the deprivations during and after the Second World War. Ernest Race was awarded the contract in recognition of his efforts producing furniture – notably the BA3 chair (see p. 32) – during this time.

Both the BA3 and the Antelope reused materials left over from armaments production – in the case of the Antelope, thin steel rods. The simple, free-flowing outline of its arms and backrail, together with the bright colours in which it was produced (red, blue, grey and yellow), gave it a friendly, cheerful feeling. The ball feet, which add to its playful appeerence, are a reference to the atomic age then gripping the world; they also anticipate the design of the Atomium building, constructed for the 1958 World's Fair in Brussels.

At the end of the festival the chairs were sold off to the visitors – as had been the case with the Landi. A few years later, such was the popularity of the Antelope that it was put into regular production. In 1955 Race exhibited the chair at the Salone del Mobile International Furniture Fair in Milan, where it won a silver medal. The red chair (opposite and pp. 26–27) is a historic model, the black chair from the current production.

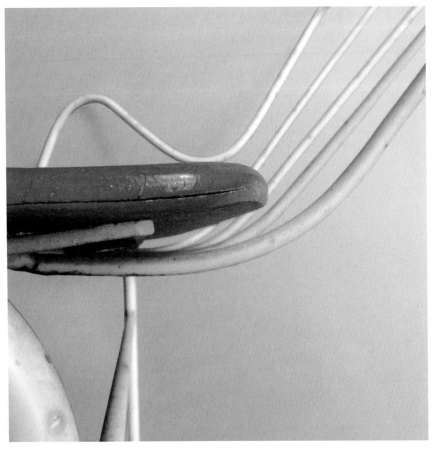

Construction

Armrests/back rail Painted steel rod
Ø ⅜ in. (9.7mm).
Spindles (vertical backrest posts)
Painted steel rods Ø ⁵⁄₁₆ in. (7.9mm).
Legs Welded painted steel rod Ø ½ in.
(12.9mm), ending in steel balls Ø 1¼ in.
(31.75mm). Each ball is drilled through
and welded flush on to the bottom of
the leg. Some versions of the chair used
plastic caps instead of ball feet; it has
been reported that cast aluminium balls
were also used. The example examined
for this book, which was reportedly
bought by a visitor at the close of the
festival, has steel balls.
Stretchers and front/rear rails
Welded painted steel rod Ø ⅜ in. (9.7mm).
Each rail has two fixing tabs 1x1½ in.
(25.4x38mm), WT ⁹⁄₆₄ in. (3.5mm), to
accept aluminium rivet. Top of rivet,
domed head Ø ⅝ in. (15.9mm); bottom
rivetted on to blackened steel washer
Ø ⅝ in. (15.9mm), WT ⁵⁄₆₄ in. (2mm).
Seat Gabon plywood moulding WT ⁵⁄₁₆ in.
(7.9mm), four drain holes Ø ⅝ in.
(15.9mm), stained red, top surface
additional clear varnish.

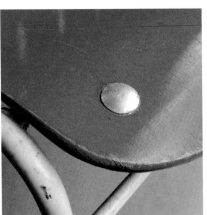

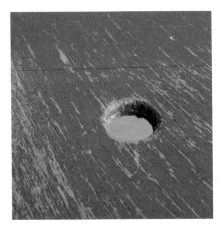

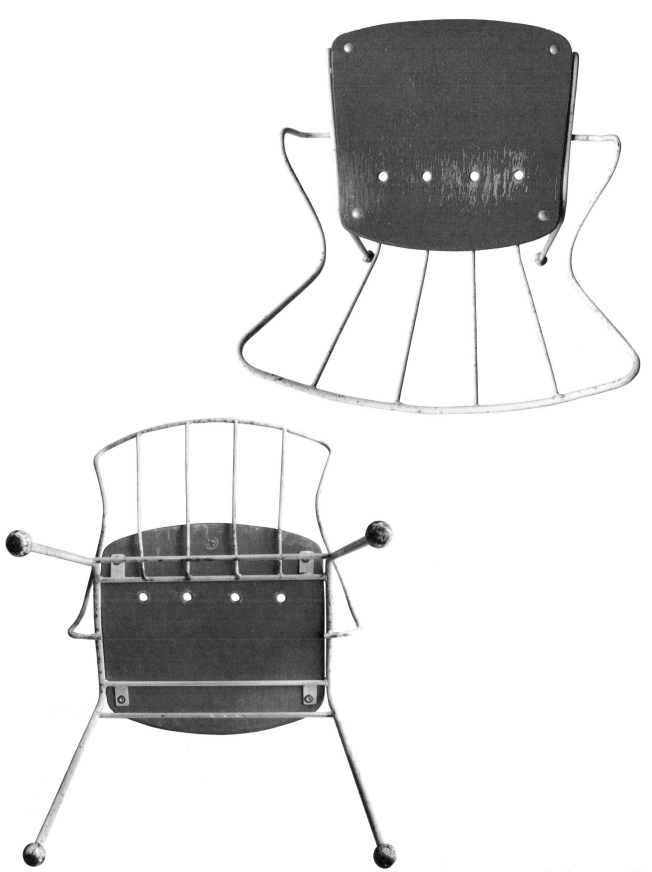

Antony

Jean Prouvé 1950–55

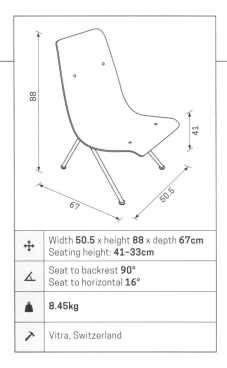

⬌	Width **50.5** x height **88** x depth **67cm** Seating height: **41–33cm**
◿	Seat to backrest **90°** Seat to horizontal **16°**
⚖	**8.45kg**
⚒	Vitra, Switzerland

Prouvé is well known for his unusual chair constructions. The Antony is no exception, with its logical and expressive metal skeleton, mixing tubular and sheet metal. Eschewing compound curves, Prouvé nevertheless achieves the impression of an organic, comfortable form. On closer inspection, one sees that the seating surface is not resting on the frame, as would be expected, but is in fact slung like a hammock between its four fixing points. The clearly defined air-gap between seat and frame reinforces the sense of accuracy and quality.

Together with the Compas table, the 356, as the Antony is also known, was designed for the Résidence Universitaire d'Antony, a students' hall of residence in Paris. At the time (1949–53), Prouvé was working closely with Charlotte Perriand on university furniture projects. The design of the chair can be seen as slightly misleading, the central tubular support of the frame suggesting that the seating angle can be adjusted (as was possible with Prouvé's 1929 chair for Louis Wittmann). Nevertheless, the low seating height and steeply angled seat offer an unexpected degree of comfort, albeit in a relatively alert position – a reflection, perhaps, of Prouvé's work ethic and his ideas about student life.

With their polished heads and distinctive pair of holes, the cap-nuts (see photos p. 30, top) can be found on a number of Prouvé's chairs. The holes emphasize the technical nature of the fixing, almost as a decorative element, but, in keeping with the requirements of public seating, prohibit any tampering with ordinary tools.

Construction

Seating surface 8mm seven-layer plywood, fixed with four drilled-spanner cap-headed nuts on to M5 (i.e. 5mm metric thread) threaded rods welded to the frame. Plywood drilled Ø8.5mm with a Ø15.5mm x 3mm sink for the cap-nut. Cap-nuts with stepped head Ø18mm very flat dome to 0.5mm edge (two Ø1.5mm holes at 8.5mm distance), then Ø15x1.5mm, shaft Ø8mm x 10mm, internal thread M5.

Legs Ø23mm steel tubing passed through and welded to single Ø50mm steel-tube stretcher.

Frame Two 4.5mm powder-coated steel plates follow the wooden seat with an 8mm air-gap, each end with a Ø48mm pressed-steel cup containing an M5 threaded rod to attach the seat.

Feet Pressed-steel cup Ø40mm x 10mm, 2.5mm wall thickness, holding a Ø34mm felt disc.

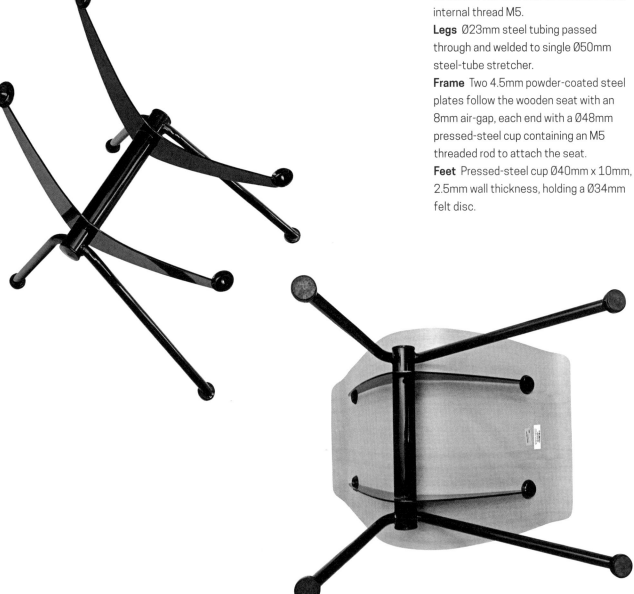

BA3

Ernest Race 1945

In 1945 Neil Jordan, director of the machine-tool manufacturer Enness Sentinel Ltd, decided to branch out into furniture production, as an alternative to the company's war-related output. Answering his advert for a prospective furniture designer, Ernest Race accepted the challenge of designing a chair without using wood, a material that had been rationed since 1942 and was unavailable for furniture design outside the government's Utility scheme.

Initially produced by means of the sand-casting process using recycled aluminium from decommisioned aircraft and weaponry, the seat was upholstered with rubberized hair and covered in dyed, recycled ex-RAF canvas duck (a lightweight cotton), in blue, terracotta or green. The front legs and the back legs were identical, so only two moulds were needed (plus one for the frame). The seat and backrest consisted of aluminium plate. Race specified a sharply angled T-section for the legs, tapered towards the feet to save material and improve the appearance of lightness.

In 1946 production was changed to the new low-pressure die-casting process (at Alumasc Ltd), originally developed for bomb casings. The metal moulds were more accurate, giving smoother surfaces and reducing both finishing and assembly costs. The greater strength of the pressure-cast metal allowed finer dimensions to be used, thereby reducing mass; the new version weighed 25 per cent less than the original, and lowered production costs by almost 50 per cent. The world's first low-pressure die-cast chair was hugely popular, selling 250,000 units between 1945 and 1964. It is still on the market.

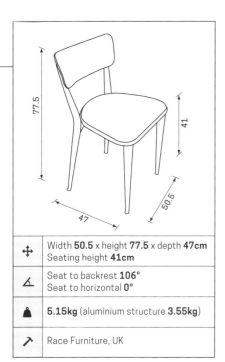

✛	Width **50.5** x height **77.5** x depth **47cm** Seating height **41cm**
◿	Seat to backrest **106°** Seat to horizontal **0°**
⬛	**5.15kg** (aluminium structure **3.55kg**)
⟋	Race Furniture, UK

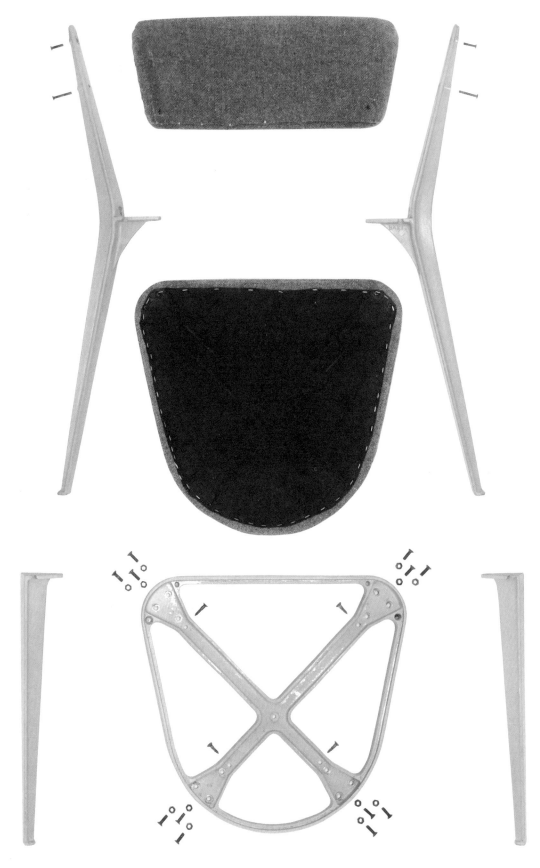

Construction

Legs Low-pressure die-cast aluminium T-section. Front leg stands vertical, 20mm wide x 16mm high at foot, rising to 44mm wide x 40mm high at top. Rear leg angled 77° from vertical, 20mm wide x 16mm high at foot, rising to 44mm wide x 38mm high at seat, then back to 20mm wide x 16.5mm high at top screw. Leg/backpost angle 151°. Central rib 4.75° draft angle. Leg brackets: WT ¼ in. (6.4mm), three ¼ in. holes, two of which are slotted sideways to enable two-part moulding (see photo this page, bottom left). Top end of rear leg: two Ø $^{13}/_{32}$ in. (10.3mm) cylinders for backrest-fixing screws (see photo this page, first column, centre). Legs-to-frame fixing: twelve ¼ in. (6.4mm) Whitworth slotted CSK-head machine screws.

Seat Edge of seat frame ¾ x ½ in. (19.5x12.7mm), rebated $^{7}/_{32}$ in. (5.5mm) to locate seat. Central cross members: U-section, base 1¼ in. wide x ½ in. high (32x12.7mm), side walls 5° draft angle, WT $^{7}/_{32}$ in. (5.5mm). Seat and backrest originally aluminium plate 14swg (WT2mm); from around 1948 (end of furniture rationing), ¼ in. (6.4mm) plywood. Seat fixing: four $^{7}/_{32}$ x ⅞ in. (5.5x22.2mm) slotted woodscrews. Backrest fixing: four $^{3}/_{16}$ in. (4.8mm) Whitworth slotted CSK-head machine screws, 2x1 in. (50.8x25.4mm), 2x1¼ in. (50.8x31.8mm) long, engaging aluminium threaded insert (see photo this page, top right).

Upholstery Originally coarse woolen weave over foam rubber, fixed with $^{7}/_{16}$ in. (11.1mm) steel tacks and staples (see photo this page, top left).

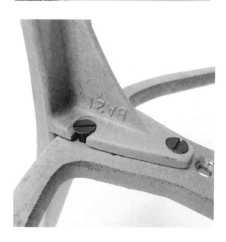

Basel

Jasper Morrison 2008

The Basel chair is a reworking of a standard wooden side chair, one of the first examples of which was the Frankfurter chair, designed by Max Stoelcker in 1935. In the case of Jasper Morrison's update, the chair is named for the Swiss city close to Vitra's headquarters in Birsfelden.

By subtly refining the curves and proportions of Stoelcker's archetypal design, and by using different materials, Morrison has brought the chair into the twenty-first century. Replacing the wooden surfaces with polypropylene brings many advantages: it enables the use of a different, more flexible construction process; the plastic elements can be mounted without screws at a later stage in production; the self-coloured material can be offered in many colour variations; damaged parts can be easily replaced; and the logo and other information can be incorporated into the moulds.

The 'fixtureless' aesthetic – no visible screws, for example – is very much in keeping with design developments in the consumer market. That the backrest tenon is slightly wider at the top, in order to conceal the aluminium-lined mortise, is an example of this (typically Morrison-like) attention to detail.

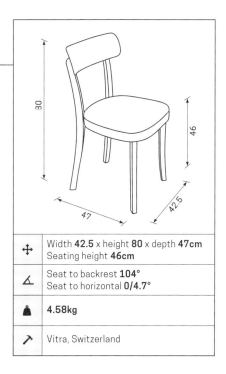

⬌	Width **42.5** x height **80** x depth **47cm** Seating height **46cm**
∠	Seat to backrest **104°** Seat to horizontal **0/4.7°**
⚖	**4.58kg**
⟋	Vitra, Switzerland

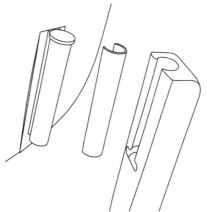

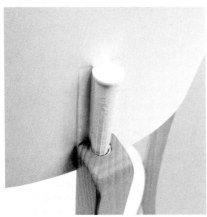

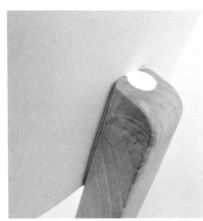

Construction

Seat and backrest Injection-moulded polypropylene, WT6.3mm. Seat edge is horizontal; central area is shaped and slopes downwards towards the back at 4.7°. Seat is fixed with eleven 3mm tabs, gripped by spring-steel clips sitting in slots in the frame. Backrest fixed with Ø10.2mm x 68mm tenon, at top Ø13mm x 2mm cap, bridge to backrest approx. 6mm, glued into slotted aluminium tube, pressed into top of rear leg.

Front legs Solid beech, rectangular section 35x26mm at frame, tapering to 27x26mm at foot. Fixed to frame with turned peg, estimated Ø20mm, glued and with additional CSK cross-headed screw from above.

Rear legs Solid beech, rectangular section 40x26mm at frame, tapering to 27x26mm at foot and top end. Slot for fixing backrest Ø13.5mm x 70mm with 9mm opening, lined with aluminium slotted tube approx. Ø12.5mm, WT1mm.

Frame (horizontal) Made up of four pieces of solid beech, 54mm high, varying width (60mm at front, 56mm at rear, 36mm at side), joined with very fine finger-joints (also known as box-joints) with 2mm pitch, 5mm height (see photo opposite, bottom). Joint reinforced from the inside with horizontal 4.5mm plywood splines (also known as 'feathers').

Blow

Jonathan De Pas, Donato D'Urbino, Paolo Lomazzi, Carla Scolari   1967

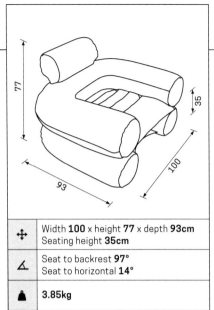

⊹	Width **100** x height **77** x depth **93cm** Seating height **35cm**
⊿	Seat to backrest **97°** Seat to horizontal **14°**
🏋	**3.85kg**
⟋	Zanotta, Italy

As the first commercially available inflatable chair, Blow embodied many aspects of the optimistic mood of the sixties. Not only was it physically light, but also its transparency and apparent frivolity introduced a totally new approach to furnishing, attracting younger people wanting to distance themselves from their parents' generation and their heavy wooden furniture. Released in 1968, it seemed to be a physical expression of the pop art movement.

The chair's innovation encompassed form, material and production, with high-frequency welding – then a relatively new process, having been invented in the 1940s – used to bond the PVC. Even the distribution was novel: the deflated chair could be packed into a small cardboard box. Also included in the box was a foot pump for inflating the chair and a repair kit (see p. 43).

Unfortunately, the PVC welds were not robust enough to guarantee a long life – at least compared to that of traditional furniture – and despite its relatively low price, its unreliabilty caused it to be taken off the market after only two years. In 1988 Zanotta reintroduced the chair with an updated packaging design, but it was discontinued just four years later. The original chair was available in clear, blue, red or yellow plastic.

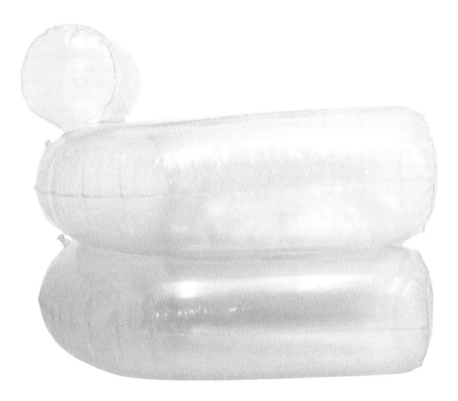

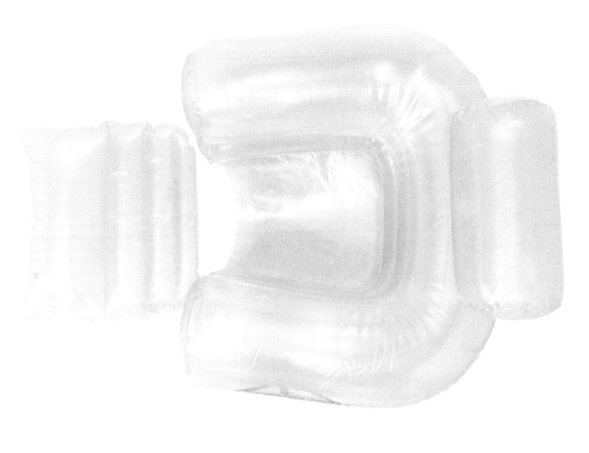

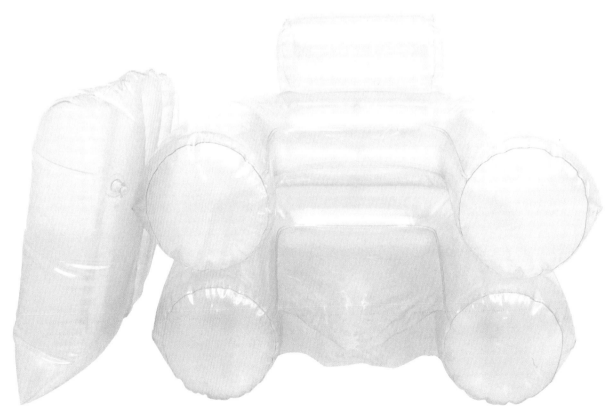

Construction

Material Transparent PVC, WT0.5mm, all joins double-welds 6mm apart.

Main body Two U-shaped tubes Ø260mm, welded one on top of the other. Seat-rest is uppermost of two parallel sheets 440mm wide x 510mm deep, 100mm apart, welded to bottom U-tube. Headrest tube, Ø240mm x 440mm long. Joining area to top U-tube approx. 500mm long x 150mm wide, perforated with one central Ø20mm hole to allow headrest to inflate via top U-tube. Separate seat cushion 600mm deep x 700mm wide, made up of four tubes with diameters decreasing in size from front (230mm, 140mm, 100mm, 70mm). Cushion is wedged between the two U-tubes, giving effective seating depth of 500mm. Useable space between armrests (i.e. air-gap) 420mm.

Main body has two PVC valves, one on each U-tube. Welding to tube Ø45mm, impressed with 'Made in Italy'. Valve body Ø15mm x 22mm high, inflating hole Ø10mm, stopper polypropylene Ø11mm x 22mm long, cap Ø17mm x 2mm. Cushion has one identical valve.

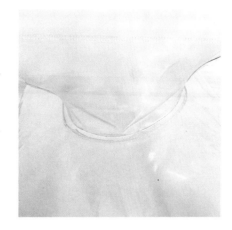
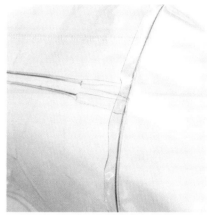

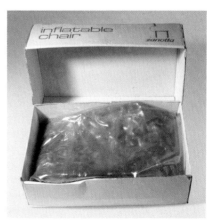

Butterfly Stool

Sori Yanagi   1954–56

Sori Yanagi developed the Butterfly Stool in conjunction with the Industrial Arts Research Institute in Sendai, Japan, drawing on the plywood-moulding experience it had acquired from the wartime production of aeroplanes (a similar transfer of technology can be seen in the early plywood work of the Eameses). In the first prototypes, the legs were cut off horizontally so that the whole edge touched the floor, spreading the load and allowing the stool to be used on tatami flooring.

In 1956 the Tendo Mokko company began producing the stool with the characteristic four-point floor contact. Over the years it has been fabricated in various thicknesses, including five- and seven-layer ply, the latter 7mm thick. Today it is manufactured by Vitra in ten-layer 9mm plywood. Tendo Mokko still produce two smaller versions – one in maple, the other in rosewood – measuring 34cm high, 31cm deep and 42.5cm wide.

The design was influenced by the Mingei (Folk Crafts) movement of the early twentieth century – an equivalent of the Arts and Crafts movement in Britain and Europe – in which Yanagi's father was very active. The stool's form is also reminiscent of a *torii*, a traditional Japanese gate most often found at the entrance to Shinto shrines, and the Japanese character 天 (heaven). Yet the stool's seating position, raised above the floor, is a Western custom unknown in Japan, indicating the growing influence of Western culture in postwar Japan.

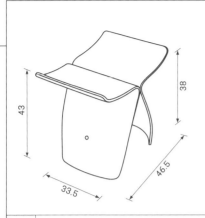

⊕	Width **46.5** x height **43** x depth **33.5cm** Seating height **38cm**
∠	Seat to back **N/A** Seat to horizontal **0°**
🏋	**3.3kg**
↗	Vitra, Switzerland

Construction

Seat Two identical moulded-plywood shells, WT approx. 9mm, ten layers of wood grouped from top side down 1-4-1-3-1, outside and centre being rosewood veneer running longitudinally, the others laid at 90° to the length, facilitating the moulding process at the tight central radius. The thickness of each shell varies between 8.5mm in the radius between seat and leg to 9.6mm in the centre of the seating surface and 8.8mm at the curved-up side-edge. From the 1990s onwards, Tendo Mokko used metal press moulds instead of wooden, resulting in more accurate mouldings.

Radius of curving-up at sides of seat R40mm; central radius between seating surface and leg R30mm; corner radii seat R20mm; corner radii leg (i.e. feet) R18mm. Front-to-back curve at bottom of legs approximately 35° ellipse. Angle between outside leg and underside of seating surface approx. 63°. Angle of leg cut-off to floor approx. 22°.

Shells drilled three times Ø7.3mm for fixing screws. Two shells joined directly without spacers using two brass slotted cap-headed M5 x 16.5mm nuts and screws. All heads Ø13mm x 3.5mm, nut shaft Ø7mm, positioned symmetrically 170mm apart. In addition, one brass stretcher rod Ø9mm x 240mm, each end brazed on triangular brass tabs 27x17mm, WT2mm, drilled Ø7.5mm, angled at 30°. Rod fixed with brass domed M5 cap-nuts Ø14mm, 3mm dome height, shaft Ø7mm x 9mm, matching brass dome-headed slotted M5 x 11mm screws. Slotted screws face inwards, non-slotted domes outwards, positioned centrally 130mm from bottom edge.

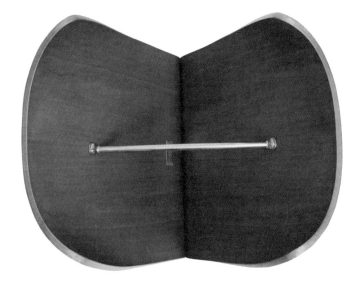

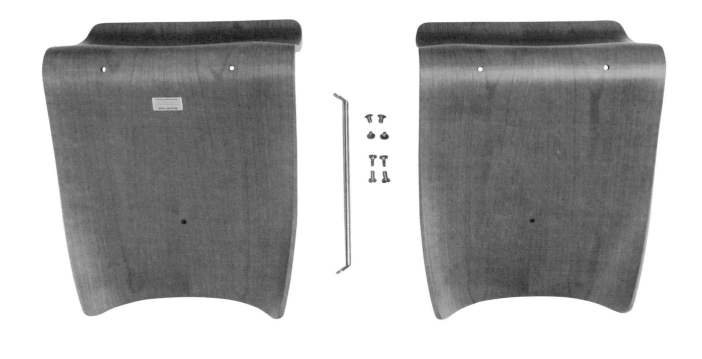

Cab

Mario Bellini 1977

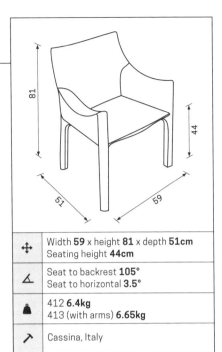

✛	Width **59** x height **81** x depth **51cm** Seating height **44cm**
◿	Seat to backrest **105°** Seat to horizontal **3.5°**
⬤	412 **6.4kg** 413 (with arms) **6.65kg**
⟋	Cassina, Italy

The Cab demonstrates the positive results that can derive from a transfer of ideas between two apparently disparate fields – in this case, fashion and furniture design. To clothe the bare bones of the chair, Bellini used not textiles but standard saddle leather, creating an aesthetic previously unseen. The 412 is produced without arms, the 413 with.

Construction

Frame Welded steel tube with bean-shaped section, widest dimensions 29.5x19.5mm, WT1.5mm. Joint between front leg and stretchers reinforced with Ø5mm steel rod in V-shape triangulation 50mm long. Rear legs surprisingly without this reinforcement. Each leg has Ø17mm steel plug spot-welded into bottom end, threaded M6 to receive foot screw, holding leather tabs together and fixing nylon foot Ø20mm x 5mm with M6 x 40mm CSK cross-headed screws, Ø12mm head.

Each foot has a Ø17.5mm x 2mm rebate on top edge (towards leather) to engage a Ø24mm x 6mm black nylon cap. The cylindrical sides of the cap, WT2mm, are split four ways to enable them to snap on to the foot. Top of rear legs (and the front legs in the armrest version) are plugged with a flexible polypropylene stopper, which sits 30mm deep in the tubes. Front stoppers 15mm high, rear stoppers 55mm, tapering to a blunt edge. These stoppers prevent the metal tube cutting through the leather during use; the rear stoppers also improve the flex of the top edge of the backrest.

Seat In early versions, the seating surface was reinforced by a simple, flat square of glassfibre, approx. WT1mm, which was glued to the underside of the leather and sat on top of the stretchers. In the present version, this plate has been replaced by a more complex polypropylene moulding, which incorporates a pad of polyurethane foam, 35mm thick, tapering to the sides.

The saddle leather, approx. WT3mm, is fixed to the frame by four heavy-duty zips and the four foot screws; the 413 has additional rivets to attach the back of the seating surface to the rear stretcher. In the case of the 412, the leather makes up 3.4kg of the chair's total weight.

Cesca (S 32)

Marcel Breuer, artistic copyright Mart Stam   1929/30

The similarities between this chair, originally called the B32, and Mart Stam's S 33 (p. 156) led to a three-year legal battle between the owner of the copyright to Stam's designs and the manufacturer Thonet, with Stam being legally recognized as the originator of the cantilever idea in 1932. Breuer's version combines the familiar features of the traditional Thonet chair – steam-bent beech with rattan surfaces – with the then revolutionary use of a cantilevered steel-tube frame.

In the United States, the chair is made by Knoll and called the Cesca. It was given this name – a reference to Breuer's daughter Francesca – by the Italian designer and manufacturer Dino Gavina when his firm, Davina, reissued Breuer's B32 and B3 in 1962. Six years later Gavina was taken over by Knoll, which has continued production to this day. In Germany, the rights to the chair are held by Thonet, which has been fabricating it under the name of S 32 since 1932 (the version with arms is called the S 64).

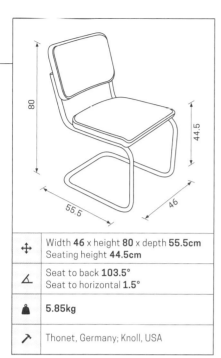

✛	Width **46** x height **80** x depth **55.5cm** Seating height **44.5cm**
∡	Seat to back **103.5°** Seat to horizontal **1.5°**
⚖	**5.85kg**
⚒	Thonet, Germany; Knoll, USA

Construction

Seat Beechwood frame, composed of four pieces of rectangular section 31mm high x 33mm wide. Front-to-side joints butted with hidden dowels; sides to rear joined in the curve with finger-joints, 4mm pitch, 10mm deep. Frame fixed to steel tubes with four 4x45mm CSK cross-head woodscrews with Ø10mm stepped nylon washers.

Backrest Beechwood frame, roughly circular section Ø30mm, joined in the four corners with finger-joints, also 4mm pitch, 10mm deep. Frame fixed to steel tubes in same manner as seat frame, no washers.

Seating surfaces Rattan.

Legs Chromed steel tubing Ø25.4mm, WT2.2mm, form-bent with 65mm inner radius on all corners. Front side of top end of tube has a formed depression 35mm long, 15mm wide, 3mm deep, approx. R15mm, to locate wooden backrest (see photo this page, bottom left). Tubes also drilled with Ø5mm front side, Ø7mm CSK rear side for the screws.

Tube ends closed with chromed, moulded ABS caps Ø25.4mm, visible edge 2mm, domed, rising to 3.2mm, 14.5mm depth into tube, Ø20.4mm with WT2.5mm. Four small 1mm ribs to improve the grip inside the metal tube.

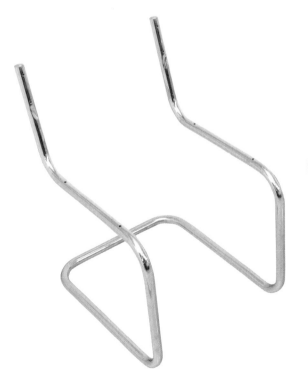

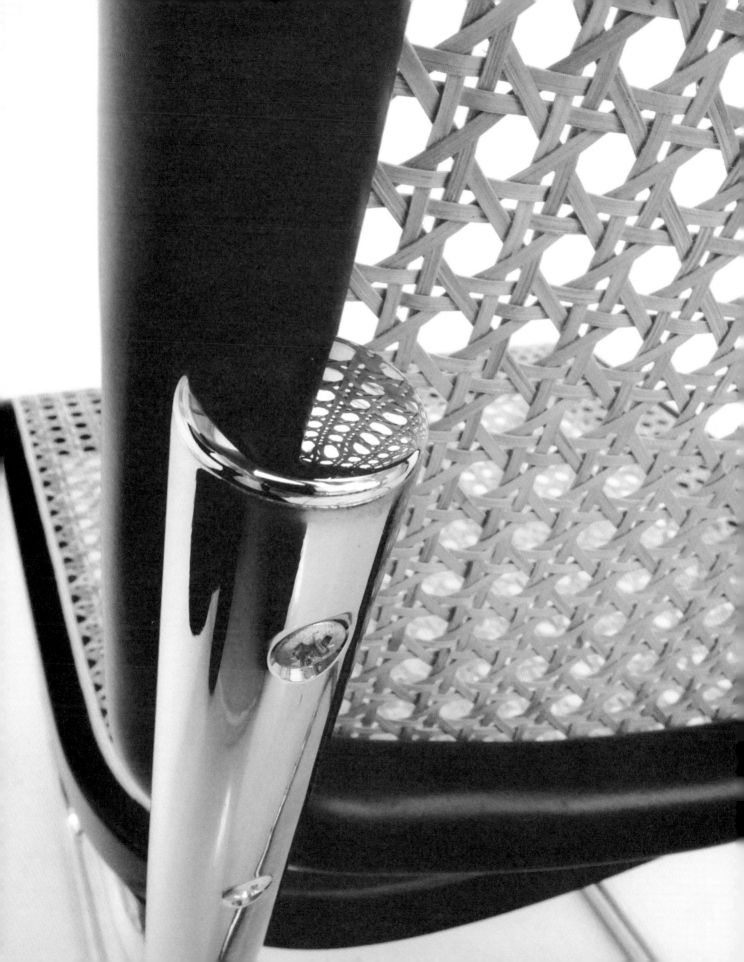

Chair One

Konstantin Grcic 2004

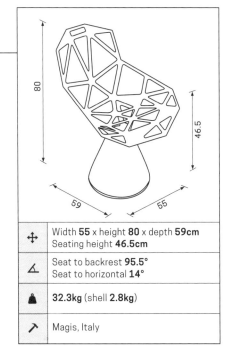

↔	Width **55** x height **80** x depth **59cm** Seating height **46.5cm**
∡	Seat to backrest **95.5°** Seat to horizontal **14°**
🏋	**32.3kg** (shell **2.8kg**)
➚	Magis, Italy

Konstantin Grcic based the design of Chair One on that of a modern football with its geometric leather panels. Yet despite the chair also being offered as a multiple-seating unit (Beam One), it was not intended as stadium seating. Manufactured from aluminium using the pressure die-casting process, the one-piece seating shell has been reduced to a lattice of differently shaped 'windows', filled only where the constraints of construction or ergonomics require. With its weatherproof materials, it was primarily designed for short periods of sitting outdoors. Indeed, the somewhat limited comfort provided by the widely spaced metal strips discourages longer usage. (To overcome this problem, Magis also offers a choice of dedicated cushions.) A range of leg types is available, including one that allows the chair to be stacked.

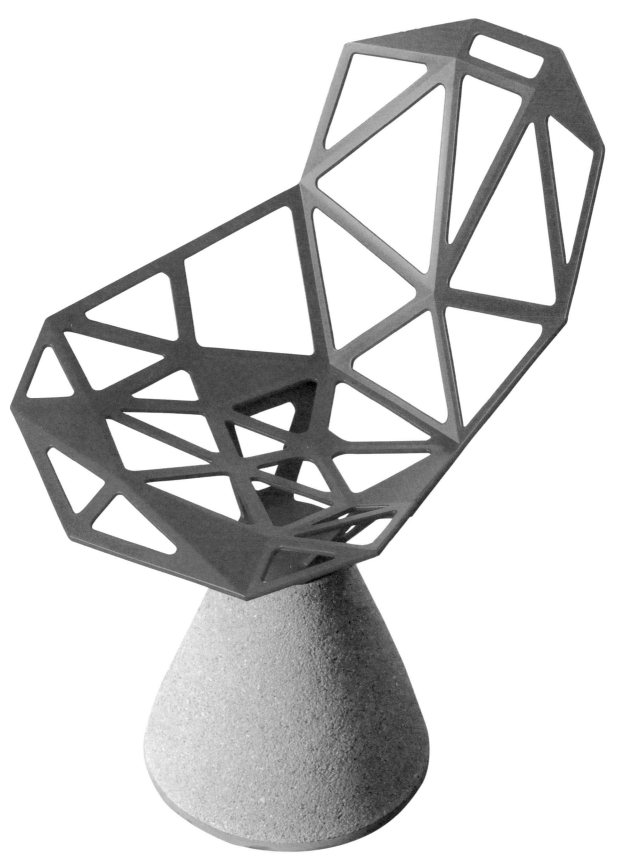

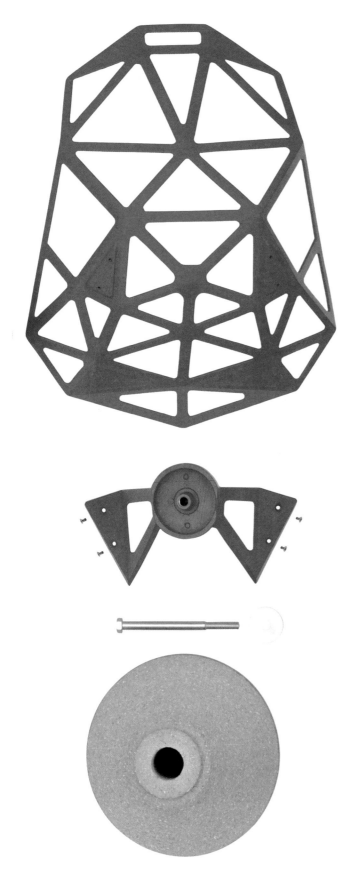

Construction

Seating shell Aluminium high-pressure die-casting WT6mm, sidebars (armrests) WT5.5mm. Strips 21–21.5mm wide, corner radius of open triangles R5–6mm. Two 5mm raised triangular surfaces, each with two tapped blind holes M6 locating the lower supporting 'wings'. The parting lines of the dies are visible on some of the edges.

Support between shell and foot Aluminium die-casting, four struts WT6.5mm, two triangular platforms WT11mm with 5mm-deep triangular recess to locate seating shell, drilled twice with Ø7mm. Attached to shell with four M6 x 10mm CSK socket head stainless-steel screws, secured with blue threadlocker. Base of support Ø125mm x 24mm high, WT side wall 8mm, top 6mm. Central boss on underside Ø27mm x 36mm high threaded M16. Cylindrical side wall flattened left and right where strut outer surface joins ring. Flats vertical but not parallel, WT at thinnest point 2.5mm. Fixed to foot using one stainless-steel M17 x 270mm bolt, 24mm hexagon head, and stainless-steel Ø64mm x 4mm washer, internal hole Ø17mm.

Foot Cement casting, surface washed before fully cured to reveal structure. Ø348mm at base, Ø130mm at top shoulder, locating ring on top Ø105mm, with central hole Ø50mm. Height to shoulder 285mm. Cement cast on to a stepped white polypropylene (PP) tube and a grey PP base. Tube 225mm long, top section Ø52mm x 190mm, bottom section Ø95mm x 90mm. Base Ø348mm, WT5mm, edge radius R12mm, 18mm high, six oval holes 42x25mm, and three Ø9mm.

Surface treatment The aluminium castings are either treated with sputtered fluorinated titanium before being given a semi-gloss powder coating in red, white or silver, or they are polished and lacquered.

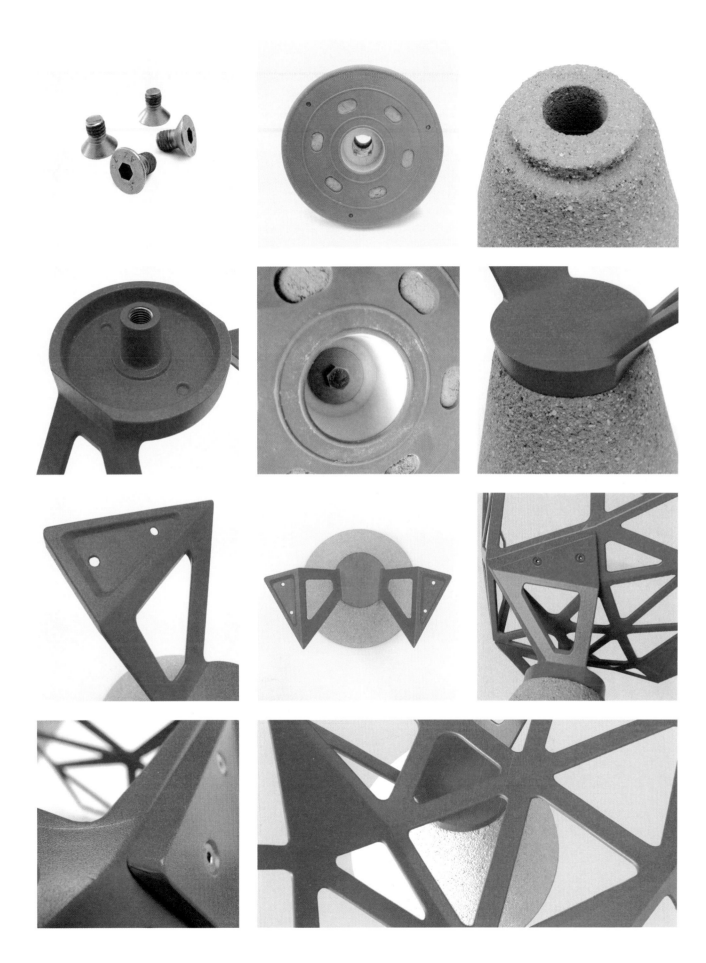

Chaise Longue (LC4)

Charlotte Perriand, Le Corbusier, Pierre Jeanneret   1928

For the 'Équipement Interieur d'Une d'Habitation' – an installation at the 1929 Salone d'Automne in Paris consisting of a fully furnished modern apartment, co-created with Charlotte Perriand and Pierre Jeanneret – Le Corbusier envisaged nine different seating types for men and women. The Chaise Longue Basculante was designed to realize type no. 4: the fully reclining seat for women. As the member of the design partnership responsible for furniture and furnishings, Perriand created a fully adjustable but non-mechanical chair by separating the design into two parts. The frame (*balancelle*) can be slid longitudinally on the rubber-covered rollers to offer many different configurations. The headrest can be as low as 44cm, with the feet above the head, or as high as 84cm. The frame can also be lifted off the base and used as a rocking chair.

The base is made of an ovoid metal tube that Perriand had discovered in an aviation catalogue. In 1929 Perriand patented the chair's design. On the patent itself (No. 672.824), Perriand's name appears

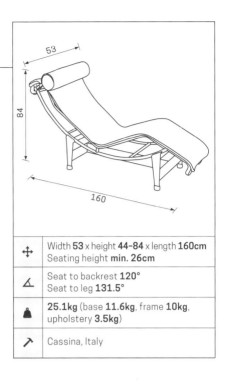

✥	Width **53** x height **44–84** x length **160cm** Seating height **min. 26cm**
◿	Seat to backrest **120°** Seat to leg **131.5°**
⬤	**25.1kg** (base **11.6kg**, frame **10kg**, upholstery **3.5kg**)
⚒	Cassina, Italy

first, followed by those of Le Corbusier
and Jeanneret. Between 1939 and 1937,
when the chair was produced by Thonet, Le
Corbusier insisted that the names be listed
alphabetically, i.e. with himself first; when
it was re-issued in 1959, Le Corbusier
ensured that his partners were not named
at all. Cassina took over production in
1964, calling it simply LC4.

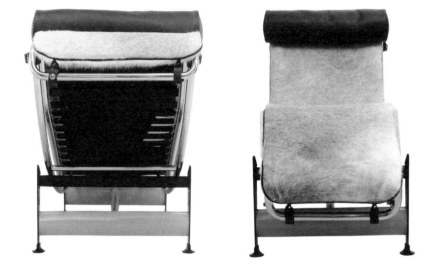

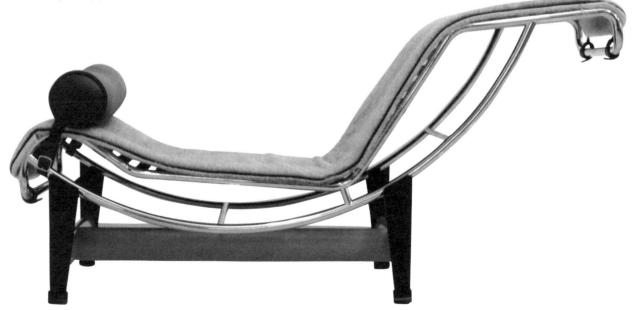

Construction

The chair illustrated here and on the previous pages is a modern re-edition of the 1928 version made for the Villa Church in Ville-d'Avray, France.

Movable frame Chromed steel tube Ø25mm, WT 2mm, outside-corner radii R60mm, main 'rocker' radius R800mm, headrest radius R110mm, radius between backrest and seat R80mm. Made in two halves joined in four places at the centre of the stretchers and head- and foot-rails using internal tubes and M6 socket grub-screws.

Stretchers Two vertical spacers at centre of rockers Ø20mm, 33mm long. Frame width at head end 530mm, at foot end 390mm.

Seating support 36 webbing straps, varying in length in 10mm steps from 440mm to 325mm, three pieces per length, 30mm wide. Held by blue-chromate steel Ø2.5mm wire hooks, locating into Ø ⅛ in. (3.1mm) holes, spaced at 1 in. (25.4mm) distance.

Base 910mm long, 568mm wide at head end, 560mm wide at foot end, measured to outside edges of the legs. H-shaped structure, welded oval-section sheet-steel tube (Perriand's *tube d'avion*) 90x37mm, section approx. a 25° ellipse. The Thonet-produced version of the chair (known as the B306 Chaise Longue à Position Variable) used a simpler, elongated-hole section with parallel sides.

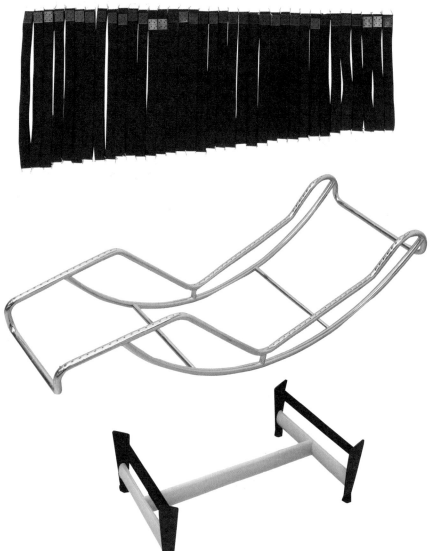

Legs Steel plate WT6mm, 310mm high, 70mm wide, tapering to 41.5mm at foot, drilled and threaded three times M4 to attach roller-fixing. Radius bottom corners R17.5mm, top corner R7.5mm. Outside edges vertical, inside edges sloping 7° towards chair centre. Inside faces above roller-fixing covered in black felt WT1mm.

Rollers Unfinished-steel tube Ø30mm, WT2mm, front 484mm long, rear 548mm, covered with Ø41mm rubber tube, WT5.5mm. Steel tube push-fitted on to Ø25mm support, WT1.5mm, 25mm long, whose base Ø60mm, WT1.5mm, is attached using three M4 x 9mm cross-headed CSK screws to inside face of legs. The rollers can rotate with a fair degree of friction on their supports.

Feet Black polypropylene Ø47.5mm, 31mm high, 6mm slot, WT3mm.

Upholstery This version: pony hide attached with black leather straps, with poppers and buckles (headrest).

Chippensteel

Oskar Zieta 2006

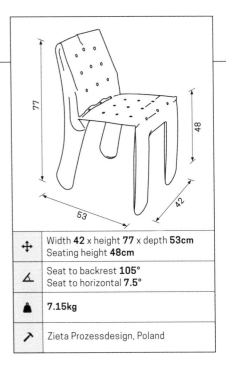

✛	Width **42** x height **77** x depth **53cm** Seating height **48cm**
⊿	Seat to backrest **105°** Seat to horizontal **7.5°**
⬛	**7.15kg**
↗	Zieta Prozessdesign, Poland

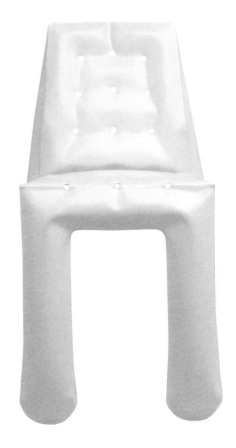

Oskar Zieta's series of sheet-metal furniture is a product of his experiments into lightweight structures at ETH Zurich, where he studied for a PhD in the Department of Computer-Aided Architectural Design. It was at ETH that he developed the FiDU (free inner-pressure deformation) process, in which flat, sheet-metal objects are inflated using pressurized air. The degree to which the object inflates – its third dimension – is controlled only to a certain extent by the outline of the two-dimensional parts.

The blanks are laser-cut out of two sheets of metal (steel, copper or aluminium), which are then laser-welded along their outside edges. Using a compressor, air is introduced (early experiments also used water) and the pressure increased until the desired degree of inflation is reached. Additional bending and small welding operations stabilize the final form. One of Zieta's goals is to create shapes that arrive at their final form through inflation alone.

The first item in the series was Plopp, a three-legged stool. Since then, Zieta has extended the collection to include a wide range of objects, such as mirrors, 'bionic' tables, hangers and large-scale sculptures.

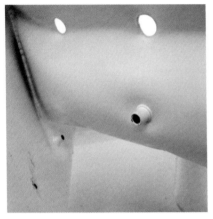

Construction

Main body Sheet steel WT1mm, laser-cut and -welded, three threaded rivet inserts M6, Ø9mm x 9mm high, to feed in compressed air (one in each back leg, one on underside of seatrest). In the series version, the back legs are inflated separately, being sealed off from the central body with a welding line, which forms the joint between backrest and leg-post. Powder-coated in white, but also available in other colours as well as other materials (highly polished inox stainless steel, aluminium and copper).

Feet Radius R60mm, reinforced with WT2mm segment running around the foot-radius to spread the load on sensitive surfaces, 120mm long x 11.5mm wide in centre.

Front legs 117mm wide at foot, tapering through inflation to 95mm wide x 66mm thick at narrowest point approx. halfway up.

Back legs 117mm wide at foot, tapering through inflation to 100mm wide x 64mm thick at narrowest point halfway up to seat, 71mm thick at seat.

Seat 'Cushions' 35.5mm thick at side, 15.5mm thick in centre area, pierced with twelve holes Ø12mm.

Backrest 25mm thick at sides, 14.5mm thick in centre area, pierced with nine holes Ø12mm.

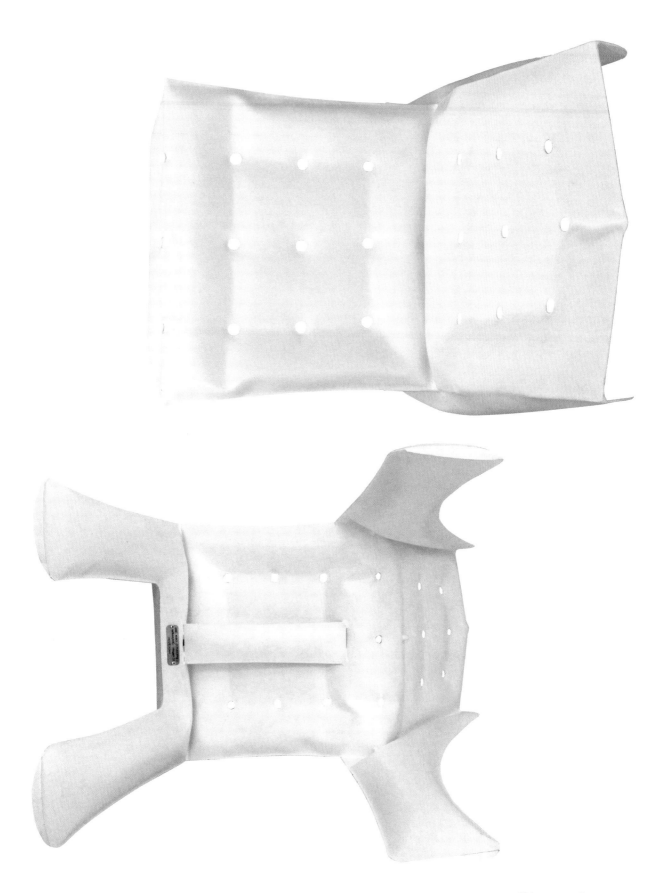

Copenhague

Ronan and Erwan Bouroullec 2012

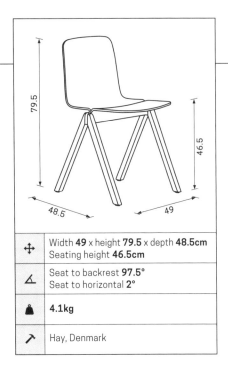

⊹	Width **49** x height **79.5** x depth **48.5cm** Seating height **46.5cm**
△	Seat to backrest **97.5°** Seat to horizontal **2°**
⬤	**4.1kg**
↗	Hay, Denmark

This chair is part of a furniture collection initially designed for the Faculty of Humanities at Copenhagen University following a major renovation. The collection includes tables, desks and a bar stool, all of which share the chair's triangular-form legs. The brief was to create a homely wooden chair, more domestic than institutional, which would create a friendlier atmosphere in the university, encouraging students not to drop out of their studies.

The chair's distinctive aesthetic is defined by the inverted V-shape of the legs, the joint simultaneously holding the legs and the single stretcher formed out of the turned-down edges of the two seat shells. This results in fewer parts, and, together with the two smaller shell-mouldings, helped to reduce the cost of production.

Prototypes of the desks and chairs had a horizontal bolt running from front to back through each leg joint. Later versions dispensed with this visible fixing, additional reinforcement being supplied by two metal rods running between the legs under the stretcher. The central-support solution also allows the two shell halves to flex more than a single moulding, improving comfort for the user.

Construction

Seating surface and backrest

10mm oak-veneer moulded plywood, eleven layers made up of nine 1mm layers plus two outside layers 0.5mm (also available in beech veneer). Radius between seat and backrest R75mm, radius across front edge of seat and top edge of backrest an extremely flat R1900mm, radius at turn-down between the two seat halves R19.5mm. The two mouldings meet in the centre to form a stretcher WT20mm. Bottom edge of stretcher drops 6mm at outside ends to match height of leg joint (60mm). Radius of stretcher to top of legs R10mm. Angle between legs 52.5°.

Legs Solid oak (or beech), 32mm wide x 40mm deep, outside edge approx. half-round radius R17mm, inside surface hollowed with R17mm, 20mm wide to improve stacking, glued and doweled at joint to seat and backrest. Area of glued surface between leg and stretcher 60x32mm. Additional stiffening: two Ø3mm brass-plated steel rods, fixing holes Ø3mm 68mm apart on rear side of legs directly under the stretcher.

Feet Nylon Ø17mm x 4mm high, snapped over metal core with fixing screw.

Surface treatment Matt laquer. Other options: soaped beech, gloss laquer, black, grey or green stain.

De La Warr Pavilion

Edward Barber and Jay Osgerby   2006

This chair takes its name from the building for which it was designed: Erich Mendelsohn and Serge Chermayeff's De La Warr Pavilion in Bexhill on Sea, completed in 1935.

One of the first modernist buildings in Britain, the pavilion was originally furnished with Alvar Aalto's 403 chair. However, this plywood chair proved unsuited to permanent deployment on the terraces and balconies of the pavilion, and had to be replaced as part of a major renovation in 2005. Edward Barber and Jay Osgerby's task was to design a modern, hard-wearing chair that nevertheless responded to the history and architecture of the building.

More than seven full-size models were made during the design process, first in hardwood, then in polyurethane foam, and later using stereolithography; one example, for a trade fair, was even milled from a solid block of aluminium. Each time the design was changed, the revisions and refinements were fed back into an increasingly complex CAD model.

The final, sculptural design refers to many of the pavilion's architectural details, such as the steel window frames, the tubular door handles, the perforated ceiling panels and the exterior balustrades. The rear skid leg creates an enclosed volume, contrasting with the hard linearity of the building's exterior. The holes in the seat and back help to reduce the chair's weight, increase its strength and minimize wind drag – an important consideration for outdoor seating.

The green chair illustrated here (and described overleaf) is an early production model. The chairs produced for the pavilion are an orange-red colour, in reference to the Aalto chairs they replaced.

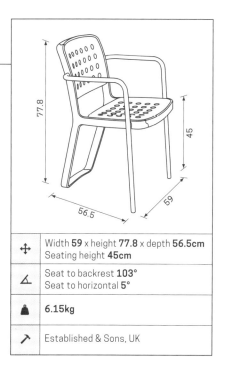

✛	Width **59** x height **77.8** x depth **56.5cm** Seating height **45cm**
∡	Seat to backrest **103°** Seat to horizontal **5°**
⚖	**6.15kg**
⚒	Established & Sons, UK

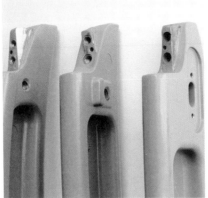

Construction

Seat and backrest 2mm aluminium sheet (sheet steel in final version), outline and holes laser-cut, pressed and swaged in two-part pressing tool, then edge-trimmed and fixing holes cut with a six-axis laser.

Seat fixing Blackened cylinder-head socket screws: nine M6 x 12mm, two M6 x 17mm. Rear four screws use nylon wedge-spacers to align, as all screw holes are threaded in one axis. Cast-on spacers at all screw holes, 1.5mm and 4mm high, ensure an even air-gap and support for the seat shell.

Backrest fixing Stainless-steel dome-head socket screws: sideways, two M6 x 40mm, which also attach the legs; upwards, two M5 x 10mm.

Front legs Ø22.5mm aluminium tube, WT 2mm (steel tube in final version, same dimensions). Legs bent with 60mm inside radius to form armrests at 660mm height. Front fixing: two M5 threaded inserts, nylon spacer (brazed-on steel spacer in final version), two M5 x 25mm slotted pan-head screws. Rear fixing: nylon compression-insert with captive M6 nut, tube-end faced at 7° angle, located in Ø26.5mm x 2mm recess in frame.

Rear legs and frame High-pressure die-cast aluminium, 44–45mm wide x 12.2–12.5mm thick, recessed sections on inside faces 8.5mm deep x 24–25mm wide. Y-shape sides joined by three stretchers, each joint positioned with wedge-tenons fixed with two M4 x 25mm stainless-steel cylinder-head socket screws (top stretcher M4 x 17mm). Screws concealed by six push-fit die-cast caps (in the final version the castings are fixed with push-fit steel pins, the structural integrity coming from the seat and backrest). To reduce costs, the frame sections had to be cast in two-part dies, resulting in each joint having different geometry and draft angles.

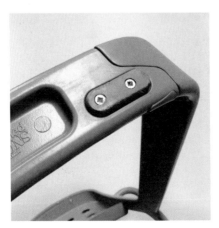

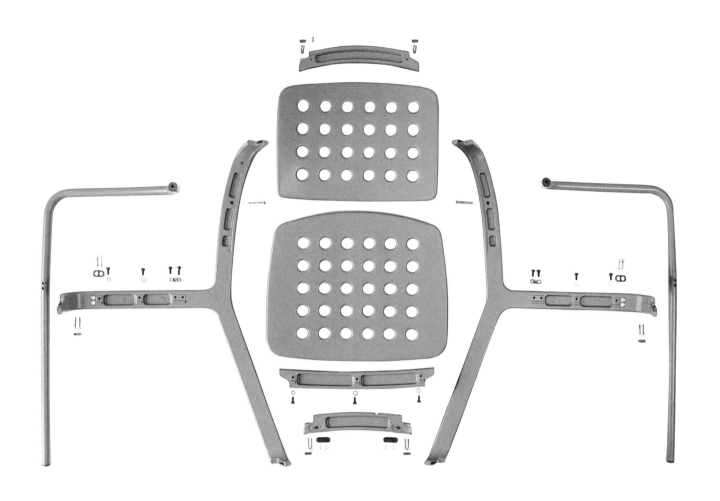

DKR

Charles and Ray Eames 1951

With the DKR (Dining K-Wire Rod), the Eameses succeeded in creating a completely new aesthetic, translating their fibreglass seating shell (as used for the DSW; see p. 80) into a different material – wire. In early experiments for their shell-group furniture, the Eameses had tried to form sheet metal using a home-made gravity press before moving on to glass fibre to help realize the complex curves they sought. Following the success of the glass-fibre shells, they experimented with steel wires, bending them to shape individually before welding them together. This avoided the problems associated with pressing and stretching metal, and allowed them effectively to 'draw' their shell shape in three dimensions.

Because it was based on the shell-group form, the wire seat could be combined with the existing base variations (cast-aluminium pedestal, swivel, tubular legs, wire struts, wooden legs and wooden rockers on wire struts). Illustrated here is the version on wire struts, sometimes known as the Eiffel Tower. As there are no shock mounts, and as the metal shell is not as flexible as the fibreglass version, the seat feels much firmer. For this reason, the chair is often combined with the 'Bikini' pad cushions, also designed by the Eameses.

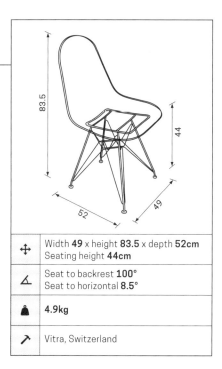

⤢	Width **49** x height **83.5** x depth **52cm** Seating height **44cm**
⊿	Seat to backrest **100°** Seat to horizontal **8.5°**
🔩	**4.9kg**
⚒	Vitra, Switzerland

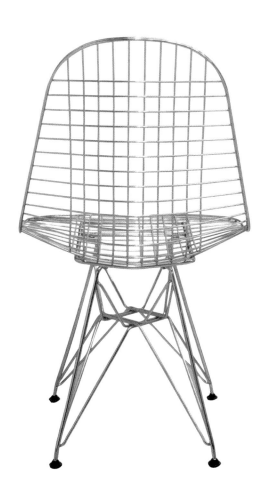

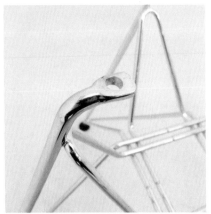

Construction

Seating surface Spot-welded Ø3.7mm steel wire, edging formed of two Ø6mm wires.

Frame Rectangular Ø10mm wire frame with two crosspieces, which are flattened and threaded M6 to attach legs.

Legs Main rods Ø9mm steel, flattened and drilled Ø6mm at top end to fix to frame, bottom end spot-welded to a Ø10mm ball to attach feet. Leg triangulation made of four diamond-shaped frames in Ø6.2mm steel, two bent upwards, two bent downwards, spot-welded to each other and to the legs. Leg-fixing screws: Ø6mm cross-headed.

Feet Ø28mm polypropylene, ball and socket, push-fitted.

Surface treatment Chrome plating.

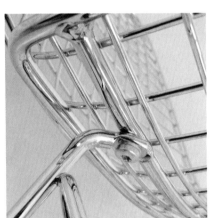

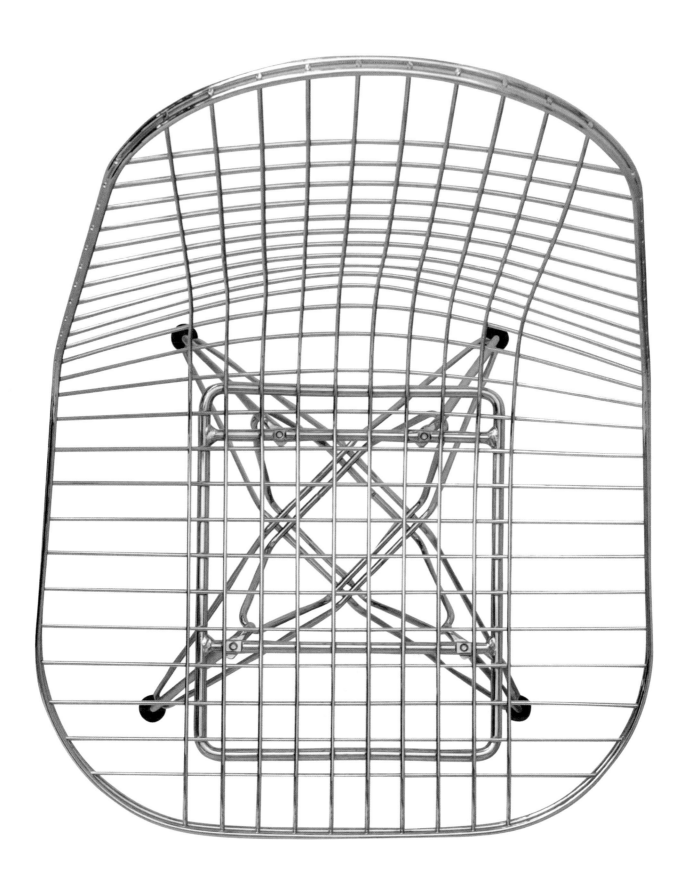

DSW

Charles and Ray Eames 1945–46

The DSW (Dining Side Wood) belongs to the series of fibreglass chairs whose development began as a result of the Eameses winning second prize at the International Competition for Low-Cost Furniture Design held in 1948 at New York's Museum of Modern Art. The Eameses' entry had used pressed sheet steel and aluminium, but the cost of tooling was so high that an alternative had to be found before the chair could be put into production. The Eameses chose fibreglass, and the result was the first-ever mass-produced series of plastic chairs.

Composed of three clearly defined materials – the one-piece plastic shell with its soft, organic form; the minimalistic wooden legs supporting the weight; the metal rods and angles connecting and stiffening the structure – the DSW is an excellent example of the fit-for-purpose principle. Each material fulfils its function according to its properties, and none could be exchanged for the other.

Over the years, a number of alterations have been made to the original design. To cope with the rigours of commercial use, the legs were reinforced with internal steel rods. And to lower costs and reduce the health problems associated with handling fibreglass, the hand-built fibreglass shell was replaced with an injection-moulded polypropylene (PP) version, whose flexibility also obviated the need for separate rubber shock mounts. The chair illustrated here is the modern PP version; for the fibreglass shell, see the PAW on p. 136.

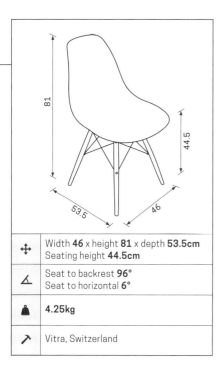

↔	Width **46** x height **81** x depth **53.5cm** Seating height **44.5cm**
∠	Seat to backrest **96°** Seat to horizontal **6°**
⚖	**4.25kg**
⚒	Vitra, Switzerland

Construction

Seat shell One-piece moulded PP, WT5mm at edge, rising to 7mm centre back, 8mm at back/seat transition, 8.5mm around and between leg fixings. Four Ø21mm cast-steel inserts, central boss Ø13.5mm, 3mm high, threaded M6, embedded in truncated PP cones: rear Ø51–29.5mm, 10mm high, total WT18.5mm measured vertically; front Ø41.5–29.5mm, approx. 8.5mm high, total WT17mm measured vertically.

Seat fixing Four non-identical 3.5x20mm steel brackets drilled Ø6mm and Ø14mm, M6 screw with 10mm hexagon head.

Legs Turned maple wood 395mm long, tapering from Ø19.5mm at foot to Ø25.5mm at middle fixing, then to Ø20mm at top fixing. Each fixing hole is drilled Ø11mm, then press-fitted with two steel inserts, reducing the bore to Ø6mm (see photo this page, top left). Outside insert is CSK to take screw head; inside is flat to meet frame. Each leg has a steel central reinforcing rod Ø10mm x 300mm, drilled twice with Ø6mm, and slotted at the top end 3.5mm wide to take the angle brackets. Leg triangulation: Ø6mm steel rods, four V-shaped elements welded into one unit, corners flattened and drilled for 6mm. Leg-fixing screws: blackened steel M6 cross-headed CSK, self-locking 10mm hexagon nuts with nylon insert.

Feet Ø17.5mm x 5.5mm PP, fixed with Ø3mm cross-headed woodscrew.

Surface treatment Seat shell: self-coloured matt PP. Legs: matt transparent honey-coloured stain (see photo this page, centre right), which results in an appearence similar to that of pear wood.

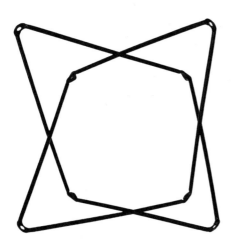

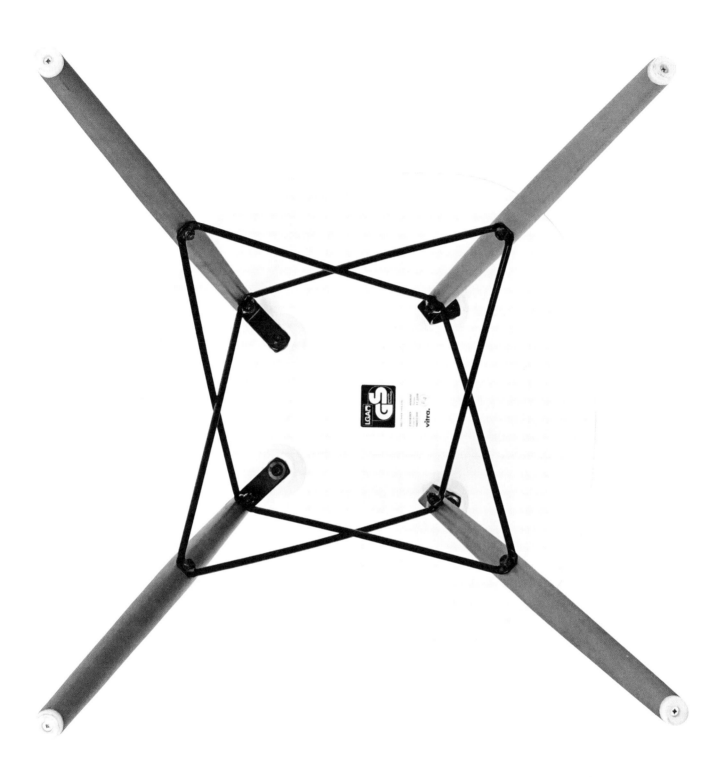

Go

Ross Lovegrove   1998–2001

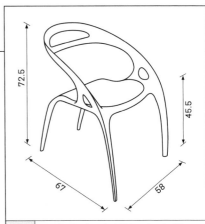

✛	Width **58** x height **72.5** x depth **67cm** Seating height **45.5cm**
⊿	Seat to backrest **108.5°** Seat to horizontal **4°**
⚖	**8.25kg**
➚	Bernhardt Design, USA

Ross Lovegrove's Go is the first chair to be commercially produced in cast magnesium. Given that this metal has only two-thirds the density of aluminium, one might expect the chair to be correspondingly light. In fact, because it is constructed out of solid castings, as opposed to having a hollow structure, it has an average weight for its size, the gracefulness of its form belying the actual amount of material used.

This aspect of the chair – its flowing, organic shape – is due in part to a secondary characteristic of magnesium. The relatively high strength-to-weight ratio of the material enables the use of longer unsupported spans, as well as legs with finer sections than could be achieved using standard aluminium alloy. The joints of the castings, which are subordinated to the external form, have complex interlocking inner surfaces that contrast significantly with the flowing outer surface. The chair can be stacked up to three or four high.

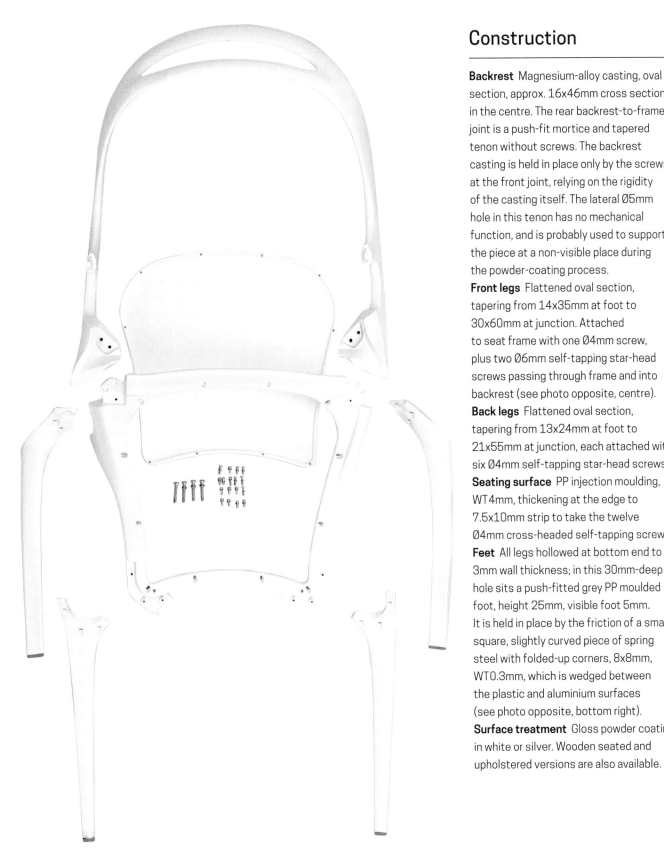

Construction

Backrest Magnesium-alloy casting, oval section, approx. 16x46mm cross section in the centre. The rear backrest-to-frame joint is a push-fit mortice and tapered tenon without screws. The backrest casting is held in place only by the screws at the front joint, relying on the rigidity of the casting itself. The lateral Ø5mm hole in this tenon has no mechanical function, and is probably used to support the piece at a non-visible place during the powder-coating process.

Front legs Flattened oval section, tapering from 14x35mm at foot to 30x60mm at junction. Attached to seat frame with one Ø4mm screw, plus two Ø6mm self-tapping star-head screws passing through frame and into backrest (see photo opposite, centre).

Back legs Flattened oval section, tapering from 13x24mm at foot to 21x55mm at junction, each attached with six Ø4mm self-tapping star-head screws.

Seating surface PP injection moulding, WT 4mm, thickening at the edge to 7.5x10mm strip to take the twelve Ø4mm cross-headed self-tapping screws.

Feet All legs hollowed at bottom end to 3mm wall thickness; in this 30mm-deep hole sits a push-fitted grey PP moulded foot, height 25mm, visible foot 5mm. It is held in place by the friction of a small square, slightly curved piece of spring steel with folded-up corners, 8x8mm, WT 0.3mm, which is wedged between the plastic and aluminium surfaces (see photo opposite, bottom right).

Surface treatment Gloss powder coating in white or silver. Wooden seated and upholstered versions are also available.

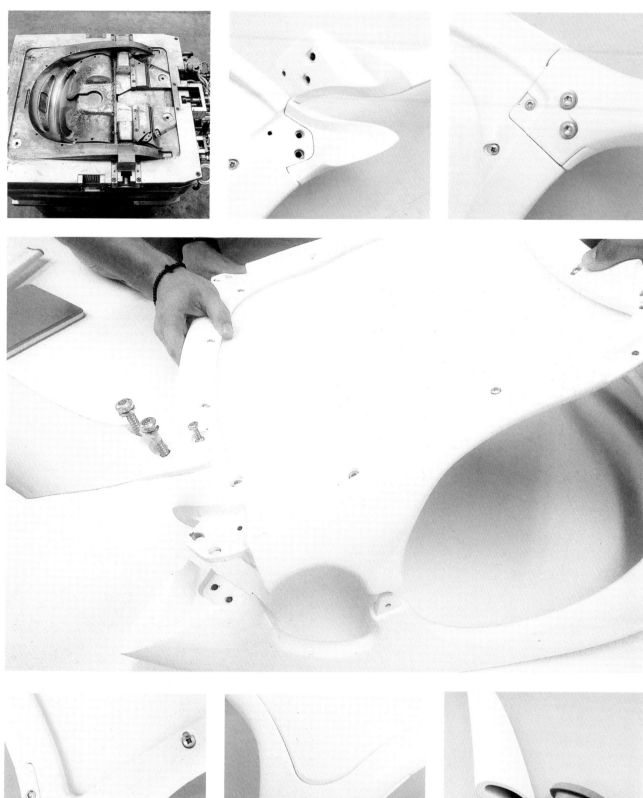
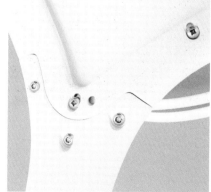

Grand Confort (LC2)

Charlotte Perriand, Le Corbusier, Pierre Jeanneret 1928

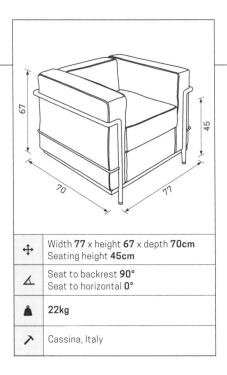

✛	Width **77** x height **67** x depth **70cm** Seating height **45cm**
◁	Seat to backrest **90°** Seat to horizontal **0°**
🏋	**22kg**
⚒	Cassina, Italy

The Grand Confort was designed to meet the requirements of Le Corbusier's seating type no. 3 (see p. 60): the semi-reclining chair for women. In response to Le Corbusier's ideas, Perriand developed what she called a *panier à coussins* (basket of cushions) in two sizes – small (now the LC2) and large (the LC3) – as well as a wider sofa version (the LC2 Divano).

By inverting the standard design of club chairs – internal skeleton surrounded by padding – Perriand achieved a modernist form in keeping with the architecture for which it was intended. Unfortunately, the tight corner radii of the external skeleton were too sharp for the tube-bending machines of the day, which meant that the frame had to be fabricated out of cast corner pieces joined to straight tubes, a time-consuming and expensive process that precluded mass production. Perriand also had a second version made with longer front legs to improve the seating angle, and another, as an alternative, with sprung rear legs, which allowed the chair to angle backwards and downwards when occupied.

The modern version of the LC2, shown here and overleaf, differs in a number of respects from the historical LC3, shown on p. 91 (bottom right). The cushions are now more geometrical, filled with polyurethane foam and polyester padding rather than down held in fabric, which softened the contours; in addition, the frame is chromed, not lacquered in such colours as chestnut brown, blue, grey and pale green. For the leather cushions of the originals, Perriand selected English leather in various shades, including biscuit, wallflower, marine blue and meadow green. A less expensive version in coloured canvas or a combination of leather and canvas was also envisaged.

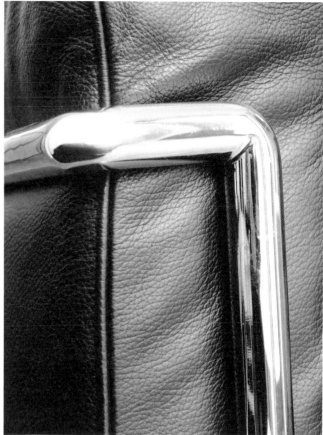

Construction

Frame Legs and top tube: chromed steel tubing Ø25mm, WT2mm, hollow corners. Middle bar: chromed steel rod Ø10mm. Bottom: chromed steel L-shaped profile 28mm vertical, 38mm horizontal, WT3mm, fixed with Ø6mm x 31mm self-tapping cylinder-head socket screws, head Ø10mm x 6mm high.

Support Nine upholstery-webbing straps 48mm wide, blue-chromate steel hook, Ø2.5mm wire, engaging in Ø7mm hole on frame.

Feet Black nylon cylinder Ø28mm x 7mm, reinforced with chromed steel cap Ø30mm x 5mm, adjusted with M8 x 25mm steel screw into a threaded nylon stopper in the bottom of the leg.

Knotted

Marcel Wanders 1996

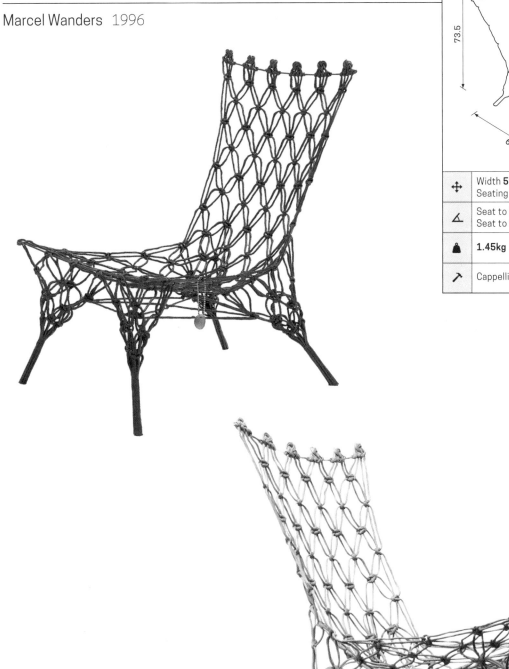

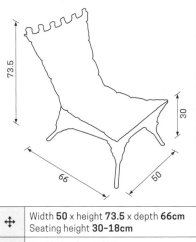

⊕	Width **50** x height **73.5** x depth **66cm** Seating height **30–18cm**
△	Seat to backrest **94°** Seat to horizontal **7°**
⬤	1.45kg
↗	Cappellini, Italy

In 1996 Marcel Wanders was asked by the Dutch design collective Droog to contribute to its 'Dry Tech I' exhibition at the Salone del Mobile (International Furniture Fair) in Milan. Interested in the craftsman's approach to the latest materials, and in experimenting with high-tech fibres, Wanders collaborated with the Delft University of Technology's Faculty of Aviation and Aerospace.

Wanders's intention was to emphasize the textile qualities of carbon fibre – to create a textile space frame combining strength with lightness. Choosing to work with aramid and carbon-fibre reinforced polymer (CFRP), Wanders wove the materials into a net-like nodal structure, which was then immersed in epoxy resin and hung in a frame to dry. The result was an unusually light chair capable of holding more than a hundred kilograms.

CFRP has ten times the strength of steel, one-seventh the weight and twice the stiffness. However, Wanders did not want a high-tech, industrial look, so – in a process devised specifically for this chair – the black of the carbon fibre was hidden inside an outer braid of aramid. In using the natural colour of the aramid and a hand-knotting technique, Wanders sought to give the chair an artisanal feel, as though it had been 'lovingly made especially for someone'. In 2001 the chair became part of Cappellini's collection.

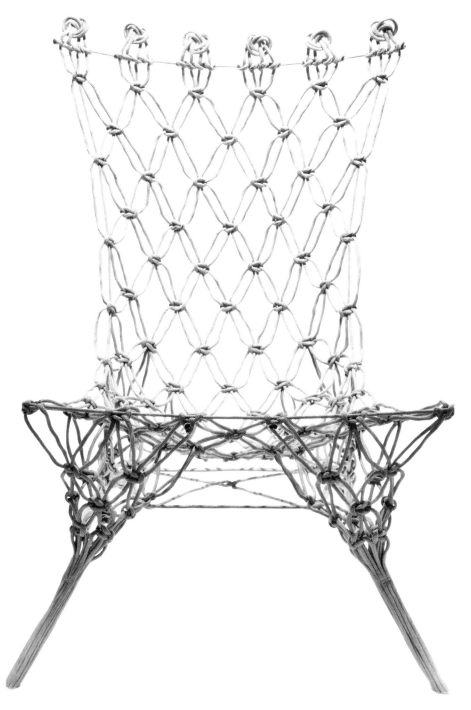

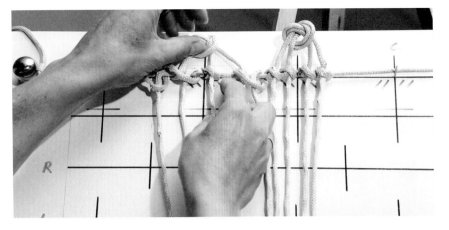

Construction

Braided aramid cord Ø4mm with Ø2mm carbon-fibre core. The main body is made up of pairs of cords knotted together in a type of macramé; the legs are formed out of sixteen parallel cords bonded together. The cord is knotted on a board, using nails on a drawing to position the knots, then the completed 'textile' is dipped in epoxy resin. Afterwards, before the resin has set, it is attached to a frame, where gravity gives it its hollow shape; in addition, the feet are pulled and tied into the correct position, while the legs are wrapped in plastic sheet and bound with cable binders. Once the resin has cured, the feet are trimmed to length with a handsaw, and the chair removed from the form. In addition to the standard, unpainted version, the chair is also available, in limited editions, in white, black or red (see photo p. 92, top), or gilded in silver or gold.

Landi

Hans Coray 1938

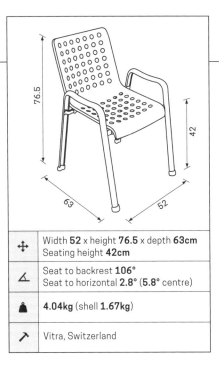

✛	Width **52** x height **76.5** x depth **63cm** Seating height **42cm**
⊿	Seat to backrest **106°** Seat to horizontal **2.8°** (**5.8°** centre)
🏋	**4.04kg** (shell **1.67kg**)
⚒	Vitra, Switzerland

Several years before the Eameses' seat-shell experiments in the United States, Hans Coray developed this design for an outdoor chair for the 1939 Swiss National Exhibition. Taking its name from the exhibition's Swiss title, Landesausstellung, the Landi was one of the first chairs to feature a one-piece pressed-aluminium seat shell. The choice of aluminium emphasized the national character of the chair, since the metal, whose production depended on large amounts of hydroelectric power, was one of Switzerland's major exports at the time.

Coray presented his design as small-scale models made of wire and sheet metal taken from tobacco tins. The chair was light, weatherproof and stackable six high. The holes in the shell reduced the weight further, their swaged edges also improving the stiffness of the shell, like a fold in a sheet of paper.

Over the years, several variations have been produced by different manufacturers. From 1962, the number of holes was dropped to 60 (6 x 10) to cut costs; later, an improved fixing between shell and frame was employed to reduce the tendency towards metal fatigue and cracking in the radius between seat and backrest. The feet also evolved, from the bare legs of the original to a wooden compound, plastic and, towards the end of the 1950s, a rubber version, all of which were intended to widen its area of use to interiors.

Construction

Seat shell Anodized aluminium WT1.5mm, punctured with 91 holes Ø24.6mm, their edges pressed down 2.5mm. Shell-edge flanged and strengthened with concealed rectangular aluminium profile 5x12mm running around circumference, stopping just after front frame fixing. Front radius of seating surface R50mm, seat/backrest radius at centre and sides R70mm, edge radius around shell R4mm, radius across top of backrest R353mm. Shell-fixing brackets: stainless-steel sheet, laser-cut 22mm wide, WT3mm, fixed to stretchers with M3 x 13mm CSK cross-headed screws, blue thread-locking agent, stainless-steel cap-headed nuts 6.7mm high, 8mm betwen flats. Brackets fixed to shell underside with semi-translucent grey adhesive. The bottom three images opposite show the historic shell-fixing on the original chair, produced by Blattmann Metallwarenfabrik.

Legs Aluminium extrusion, U-section, 33.5mm wide x 16mm high, WT6mm, internal radius R10mm, edge radius R2mm, near bottom edge pierced with square hole 7.3x7.3mm to fix foot. Legs form an inverted 'V' angle 25.3° to each other. Right and left leg-frame parallel, front legs rise 101.3° from horizontal, back legs 102.1°. Gap between armrests 430mm. Height of centre of armrest from ground 575mm.

Stretchers (cross braces) Aluminium extrusion 5.8x27.5mm, curved over their length to clear underside of shell. Front stretcher R1300mm, rear stretcher R550mm, both welded to inside of legs.

Feet Solid moulded TPE, which follows the shape of the leg profile, height 29mm, width 48mm, depth 33mm. Within curved slot, small tab to engage with square hole in leg.

LCW

Charles and Ray Eames   1945–46

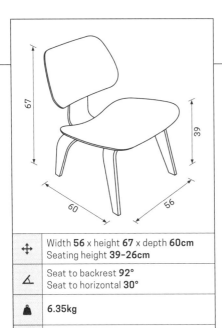

↔	Width **56** x height **67** x depth **60cm** Seating height **39–26cm**
∠	Seat to backrest **92°** Seat to horizontal **30°**
⚖	**6.35kg**
⚒	Herman Miller, USA; Vitra, Switzerland

In designing the LCW (Lounge Chair Wood), the Eameses sought to create a comfortable, non-upholstered club chair, using moulded plywood and rubber shock mounts. The latter, a patent of Charles Eames (US Patent No. US2649136), would also be used for the Plastic Shell Group (see, for example, the PAW, p. 136) and the Lounge Chair. The rubber allowed the seats and backrests to flex, improving the comfort of the non-upholstered chairs. Another advantage of the shock mounts was that they could be glued to the wooden surface, meaning that the fixings were invisible from the front.

In contrast to usual practice, the outside layers of plywood on the frame and legs are not laid at right-angles to the inside layers, for increased stiffness. Instead, they are deliberately laid in the same grain direction to aid flexibilty.

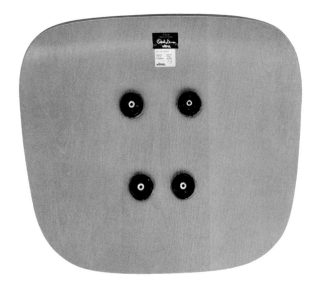

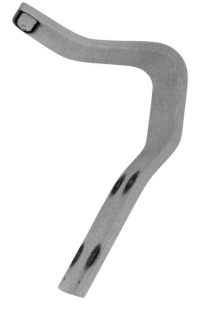

Construction

Seat and backrest Three-dimensionally moulded seven-layer plywood WT8.5mm.
Frame A complex piece of moulded plywood. The vertical section has twelve layers of wood veneer, 15.8mm thick, rising to fourteen layers with 18.3mm thickness beginning 180mm down from the top edge. The extra 2.5mm

are introduced over approx. 60mm just before the frame makes the R40mm curve to be horizontal above the back leg. The frame tapers in width from 115mm at backrest-fixing to 144mm wide under seat, drilled with six Ø6.5mm holes to attach backrest and seat, plus four Ø12.5mm M6 threaded inserts to attach the rear leg. Of the fourteen layers of plywood, four have the grain running longitudinally (including the two outside layers), while the others are laid at 90° to the length, facilitating the moulding process and improving the flex of the back. The full pattern is 1-3-1-4-1-3-1, the four central layers being reduced to two for vertical section.

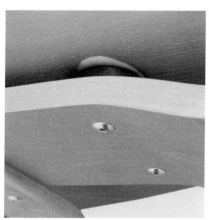

Front leg is attached using two shock-mount fixing screws, and two screws to cap-nuts on the front edge of the frame. Shock mounts are fixed to the seat with an epoxy glue, and to the frame with Ø15mm dome-headed M6 socket screws.

Legs Twelve-layer plywood 16.5mm thick, both legs tapering from 87mm at frame to 40mm at foot. The outside layers of plywood have grain laid longitudinally; the other ten are laid at 90° to the length.

Seat-fixing Four Ø30mm flexible rubber shock mounts, front 14mm, rear 12mm high, containing 4mm sheet-steel inserts drilled and threaded M6.

Backrest-fixing Oval shock mount 40x105 x16mm, with a sheet-steel insert WT 4mm containing two M6 threaded holes.

Surface treatment Matt transparent wood stain.

A dining version (DCW) is available with a greater seating height of 43cm. Two other versions have steel tubular legs: the LCM (Lounge Chair Metal) and the DCM (Dining Chair Metal).

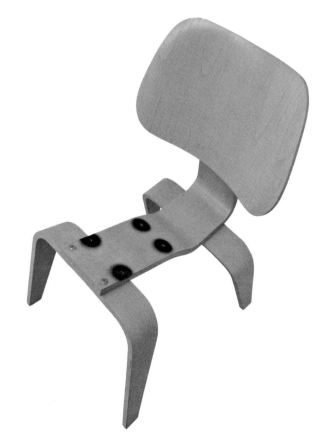

LL04

Maarten Van Severen 2004

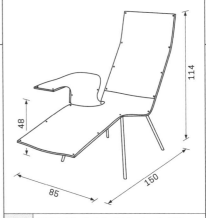

✛	Width **85** x height **114** x depth **150cm** Seating height **48–38cm**
◿	Seat to backrest **112.5°** Seat to horizontal **14°** Footrest to horizontal **10°** Headrest to vertical **12°**
⬛	**23kg**
➚	De Padova, Italy (previously UMS Pastoe, the Netherlands)

The LL04 can be seen as a development of Van Severen's CN° II side chair. The wooden ply skin has been replaced with leather, the seat extended, and the backrest angle opened up to offer a reclining position.

The chair's design is typical of Van Severen's reductionist approach: just two materials, steel and leather; the supporting structure reduced to the absolute minumum; the seating surface fixed directly and visibly to the frame. The single, asymmetric armrest is a prerequisite for the centrally placed legs, enabling the user to sit down sideways before turning and reclining on the chair.

Joost van der Vecht, the creative director of Pastoe, recalls working on the first production version. Van Severen, he notes, spent years refining his designs to achieve the best proportions and techniques, displaying a remarkable attention to detail.

Construction

Seating surface Three pieces of 5–6mm vegetable-tanned saddle leather, cross-stitched together, width 500mm, affixed to frame with twenty-five M3 star-headed CSK stainless-steel screws, head Ø8mm. For the black-leather version (see below), the screws are chemically oxidized to a black finish.

Frame Welded rectangular stainless-steel strips, 10x30mm, drilled and threaded M3. The usually non-visible holes under the armrest are drilled through the frame; the screw holes that would otherwise be visible, e.g. for fixing the leather to the backrest, are blind holes.

Legs Ø20mm stainless-steel tubing, 2mm wall thickness.

Feet Ø20mm polypropylene, 3mm visible.

Surface treatment Brushed steel, unpolished natural hide. The chair is also available in aniline-dyed black leather.

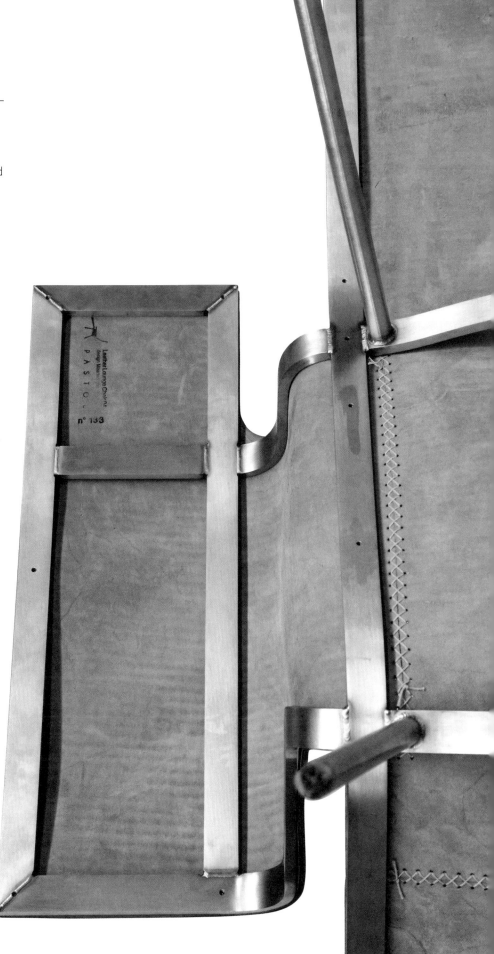

Lord Yo

Philippe Starck 1993

In addition to its unusual mix of materials, the Lord Yo is notable for being one of the first outdoor chairs to incorporate formal and historical elements of the indoor chair. Despite its outdoor credentials, the weatherproofing features are kept in the background: the seating surface is slightly raised, simultaneously suggesting a cushion and forming a gutter at its back edge, allowing rainwater to run off through the side holes. These in turn are large enough to accept the rear legs when stacking the chairs (unusually for its shape, it can be stacked up to six high).

The references to traditional indoor seating – the high, rounded backrest, the welcoming angle of the armrests, the curved and splayed legs – lend a sense of familiarity to an otherwise novel form of furniture: the inside/outside armchair. The large polypropylene shell also conceals the more technical aspects of the chair, notably the aluminium pressure casting that connects the legs to the shell, thereby underplaying the high-tech in order to increase the chair's appeal. A tailored cotton, cushioned slipcover can be used to give the chair a more traditional look.

	Width **62** x height **94** x depth **65cm**
	Seating height **44.5cm**
	Seat to back **104°**
	Seat to horizontal **4°**
	6.3kg
	Driade, Italy

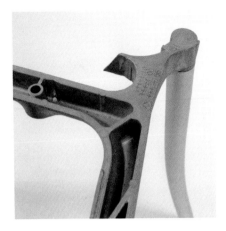
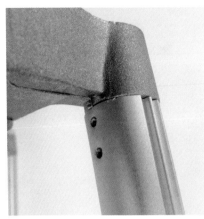
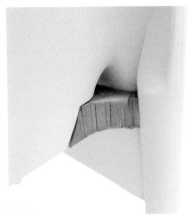

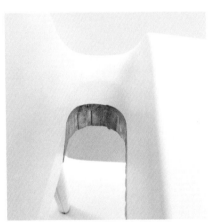

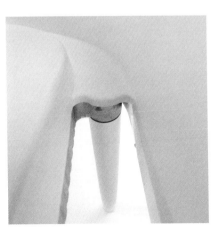

Construction

Shell Injection-moulded PP, WT4–5mm, front skirt WT3.5mm, reinforcing ribs WT3mm supporting Ø11mm screw-bosses. Fixing to frame: six stainless-steel Ø5.6mm x 33mm star T25 cylinder-head self-tapping screws. To left and right of seating surface: two slots 225mm long x 36mm wide tapering to 44mm wide at top edge to accept legs when stacking.

Frame High-pressure aluminium die-casting, WT5mm, V-section 23x23mm, drilled with six Ø6.3mm holes for seat-fixing, each with Ø10mm x 7mm recession for screw-head. Additionally eight Ø3mm holes for two clear-plastic half-round strips to protect seat when stacking chairs; strips 6.5x4x170mm, each with four pegs Ø3mm x 4mm, push-fit plus transparent adhesive.

The frame has four solid cylindrical lugs to locate legs, Ø20mm x 47mm long, each with a longitudinal depression, 9mm wide x 2mm deep, radius R6.5mm to match internal leg profile.

Legs fixed to frame with push-fit on to lugs, then each stamped twice with pointed 3mm punch, stamps 26mm apart on front legs, 9mm apart on rear.

Legs Extruded aluminium tube profile, Ø23.5mm, WT1.75mm, with curved depression 7.5mm wide outside, with 2x2mm central rib. Rear legs 394mm, front legs 372mm long, each with one large radius curve in the middle section, length of curved section approx. 180mm.

Feet PP, 15mm insert in tube, 2mm edge, domed to 5mm height with R30mm. The leg profile is matched on the tubular insert.

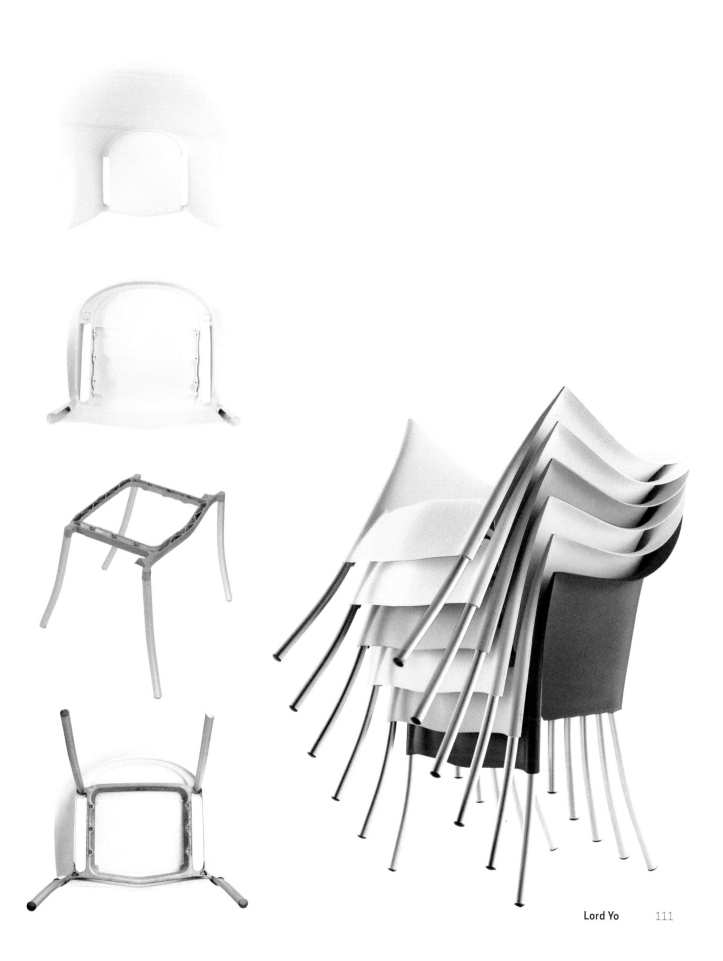

Lord Yo

Lounge

Nick Crosbie 1997

Having already experimented with inflatable structures and products as part of his master's degree, Nick Crosbie founded his own company, Inflate, shortly after graduating. Its first products included such diverse items as egg cups, vases, wine racks and furniture. Linking all these items was a central design concept: the inflation of a membrane to achieve a rigid or resilient structure. In his later work, Crosbie applied this concept to much larger objects, developing architectural components and, ultimately, inflatable buildings.

The Lounge chair combines the innovation of an inflated seating surface with a conventional supporting structure using standard components (the laminated wooden slats were ready-mades intended for bed frames). Initially, production was by hand, the individual cushions taking up to half an hour each to cut out, press and weld. The result is a previously unseen aesthetic, its combination of forms and materials suggesting an *objet trouvé* or a DIY project, yet with the quality, proportions and finish one would expect from a well-established manufacturer. Crosbie describes his approach to furniture design as challenging perceptions.

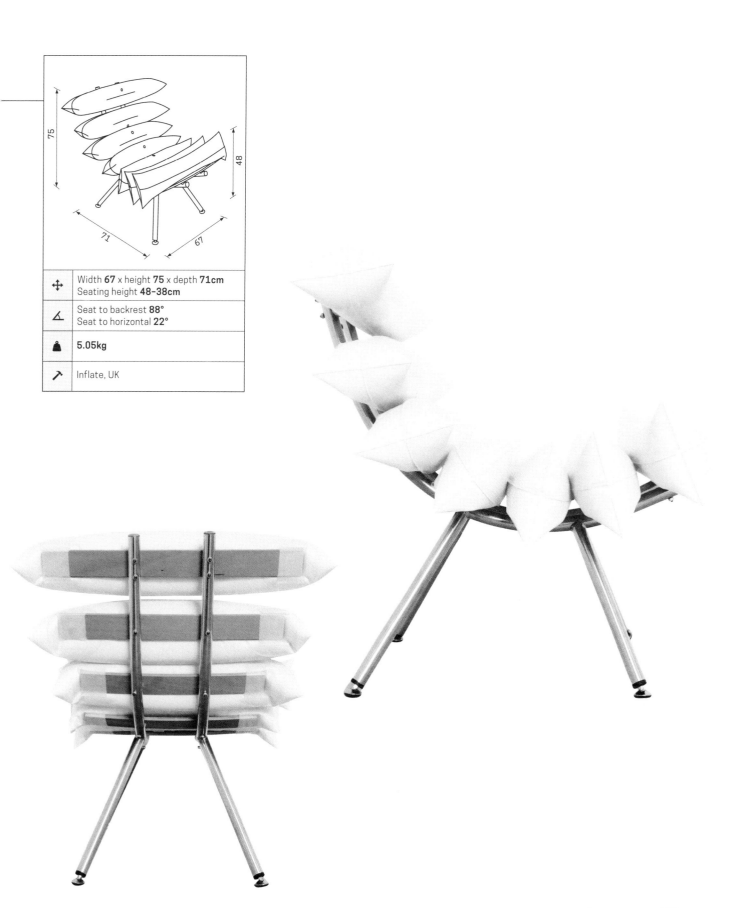

↔	Width **67** x height **75** x depth **71cm** Seating height **48–38cm**
∠	Seat to backrest **88°** Seat to horizontal **22°**
⚖	**5.05kg**
⚒	Inflate, UK

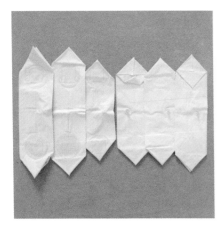

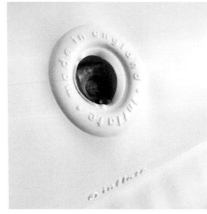

Construction

Legs and frame Stainless-steel tubing Ø25.4mm, welded joints, drilled with Ø6.5mm holes to accept M6 steel bolts. Nylon spacers between frame and slats Ø25mm, four per slat.

Slats Laminated beech, 8x53mm section, edge half-round R4mm, two pieces each of the lengths 660mm, 600mm and three of length 540mm.

Cushions Self-coloured PVC, WT0.5mm, weld WT1mm, two pieces each of 190x670mm, 190x620mm and 190x560mm, uninflated dimensions. Each cushion inflated through standard PVC valve, flat base with embossed company name Ø30mm, tube tapers Ø14mm bottom to Ø10mm top, hole Ø5mm. Each cushion has two transparent PVC pockets welded to its rear side for attaching it to the slats.

Feet Standard adjustable swivelling leveler glides, Ø31mm, chromed steel cover, ball and socket, Ø10mm, screwed with M8 into polypropylene push-fitted sockets in the bottom of the legs.

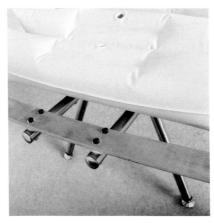

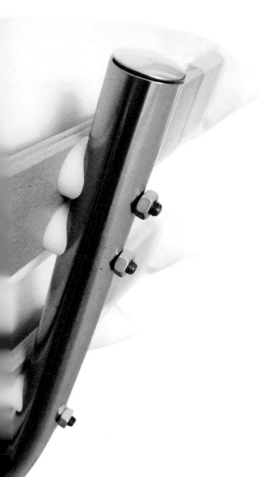

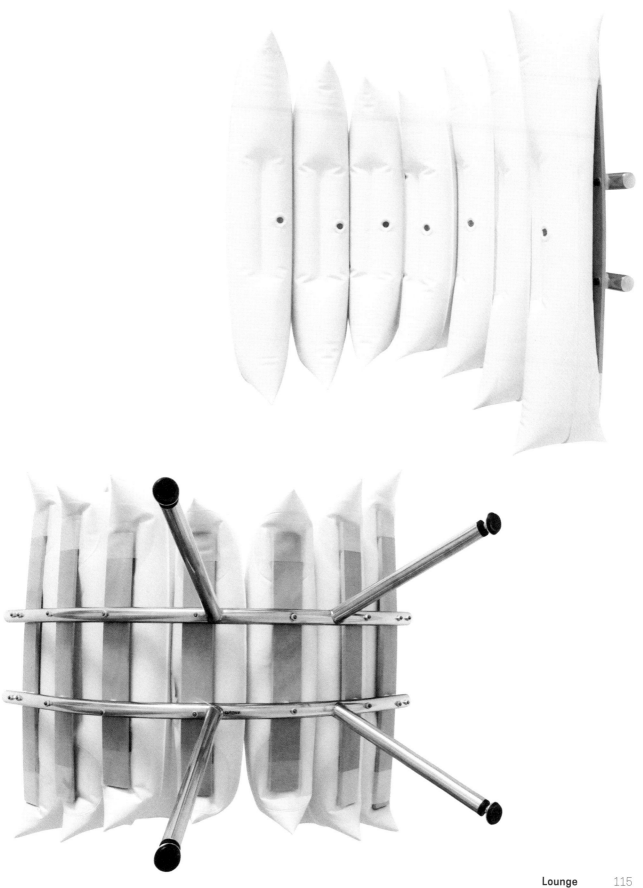

Mezzadro Stool

Achille and Pier Giacomo Castiglioni 1954–57

First put on show in 1957 at the exhibition 'Colours and Shapes in the House of Today' at the Villa Olmo in Como, Italy, this stool was deliberately assembled out of ready-mades – a 1935 tractor seat and its metal support, a wing nut from a bicycle, and a foot that resembled the rung of a wooden ladder. As yet without a name, it was intended to emphasize the Castiglioni brothers' desire to go beyond functionalism in the design of everyday objects. Their unique approach was way ahead of its time, laying the foundations not only for the Radical Design (or Anti-Design) movement of the late 1960s but also, ultimately, for the postmodernist turn of the 1980s.

The stool's current name – meaning 'sharecropper' or 'tenant farmer' in English, a reference to the use of a tractor seat – was first introduced by Zanotta when it put the stool into production in 1970. At this point, a number of changes were made to the design: a modern tractor seat was chosen, one with fifteen holes (instead of twenty-two) and a more complex form; the leg was upgraded to stainless steel; the seat was powder coated; and the foot screws were positioned underneath the wooden bar, rather than sitting visibly on top.

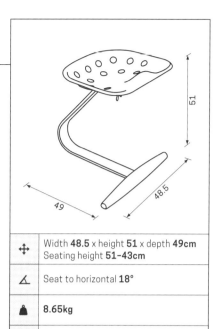

✛	Width **48.5** x height **51** x depth **49cm** Seating height **51–43cm**
∠	Seat to horizontal **18°**
⬤	**8.65kg**
➤	Zanotta, Italy

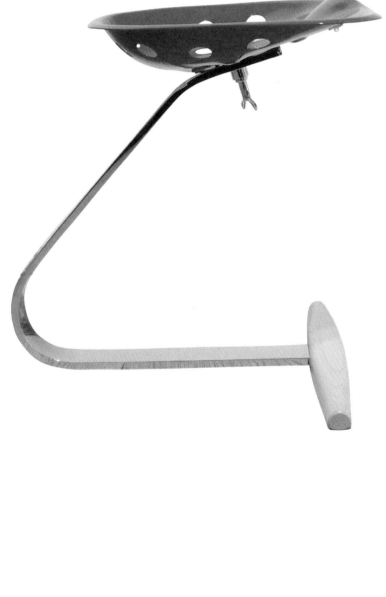

Construction

Seat Pressed sheet steel, WT2mm, powder-coated, fifteen punched holes Ø30mm, central square hole 14x14mm. Fixed with one M8 dome-headed bolt, dome Ø38mm, shank Ø12mm, black rubber washer Ø32mm x 1mm, chromed steel spacer ring Ø25mm x 15mm, with Ø10mm central hole, two C-shaped cast-aluminium spacers, 48x35mm, WT3.5mm, arm width 10mm, with two pressed studs Ø6mm x 2.5mm high to orient the spacers either side of the fixing bolt on the top of the leg. The arms of the spacers engage in the two longitudinal parallel grooves of the seat-pressing to prevent the seat turning. Bicycle wing nut M8, 65mm wide, 43mm high.

Leg Chromed steel bar, 60x12mm (originally a standard tractor-seat support used upside-down), drilled Ø16mm at top end, drilled and threaded with two M6 holes at bottom end. Approx. 35mm in front and behind of the top hole a pair of Ø7mm depressions to hold the studs of the spacers.

Foot Solid beech three-quarters round, 485mm long, tapered from 50x41mm in the centre to 32x28mm at the ends, finished in clear laquer. Morticed centrally on the side with 60x12mm to accept the bottom end of the leg, fixed with two steel CSK socket-head (1970s version, slotted-head) M6 screws. In the original version from 1957, the mortice was a slot, with the leg passing right through the foot to be visible on the front side.

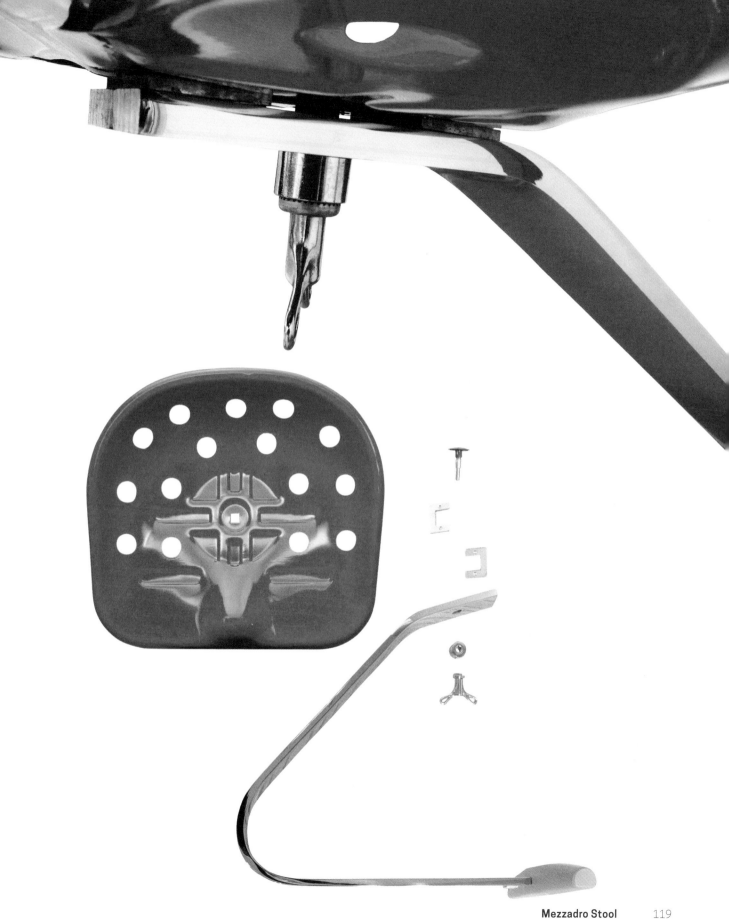

No. 14 (No. 214)

Michael Thonet 1859

The Gebrüder Thonet company received a patent for its new steam-bending process in 1856; three years later, it created the No. 14 (known today as the No. 214), the first chair to be industrially produced using the new process. By bending already-turned solid wood, the company no longer had to rely on the previously used and time-consuming process of laminating veneer and hand-finishing in order to achieve the rounded forms of the age. In about 1860, the company added children's furniture to its range, including a small version of the No. 14. The bottom four photos on p. 123 show a children's No. 14 purchased in 1872; all other photos are of the full-size, modern version produced almost a century and a half later.

The new mass-produced furniture proved extremely successful, and by 1886 Thonet's second catalogue listed more than a hundred chairs, as well as beds, tables and coat racks. The No. 14 cost 3 gulden (guilder), the matching two-seater version almost 6 gulden, the children's size 2 gulden.

The rationalization that lay behind the No. 14's production – Thonet made many different chairs out of a standardized set of parts – also extended to its distribution. It could be disassembled into six pieces (seat frame, legs, backrest, stretcher ring), enabling thirty-six chairs to be packed into a one-cubic-metre shipping container.

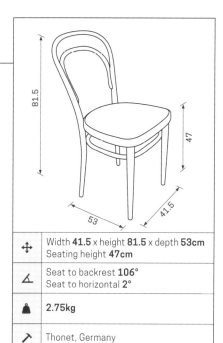

✛	Width **41.5** x height **81.5** x depth **53cm** Seating height **47cm**
∡	Seat to backrest **106°** Seat to horizontal **2°**
⚖	2.75kg
✎	Thonet, Germany

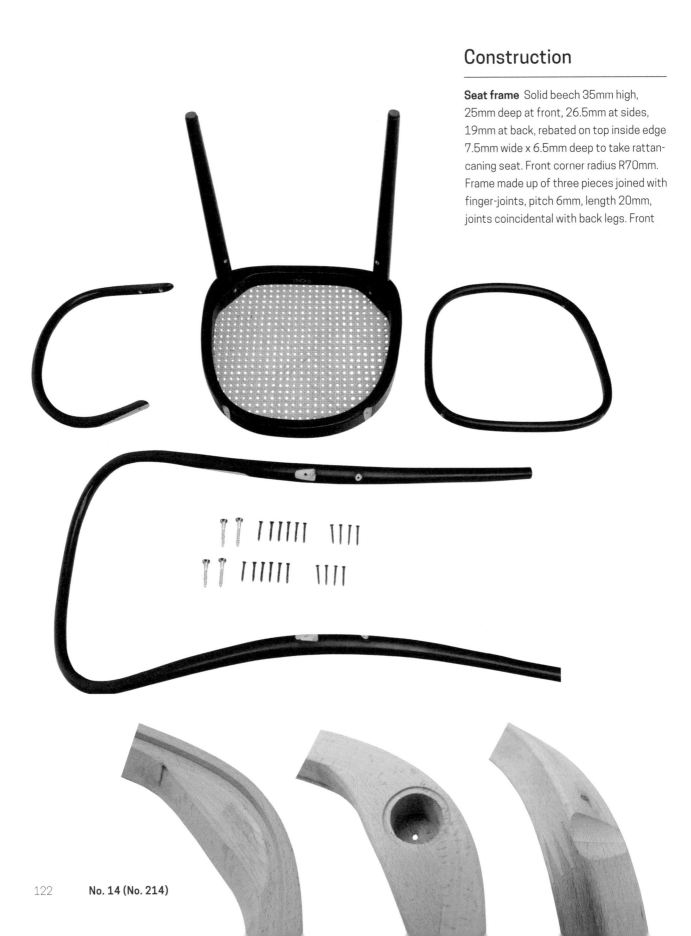

Construction

Seat frame Solid beech 35mm high, 25mm deep at front, 26.5mm at sides, 19mm at back, rebated on top inside edge 7.5mm wide x 6.5mm deep to take rattan-caning seat. Front corner radius R70mm. Frame made up of three pieces joined with finger-joints, pitch 6mm, length 20mm, joints coincidental with back legs. Front

inside corners have an additional triangle to support the leg, attached to the frame with a very fine finger-joint, 1.6mm pitch, 4mm length. The triangle is 31.5mm thick at frame, dropping to 28mm in centre to allow for seat to flex (see photos opposite, bottom). Frame drilled for front legs Ø29mm x 28mm deep with Ø37mm x 2mm rebate for shoulder on leg. Frame grooved outside with a shallow R17mm to accept back leg.

Front legs Solid beech, 450mm long, tapered from Ø22.5mm at foot to Ø35mm at seat, finishing with a Ø29mm x 26mm peg. Both legs fixed with a single Ø5mm x 36mm cross-headed steel woodscrew from inside frame.

Back legs Steam-bent solid beech, Ø22.5mm at foot tapering to Ø32.5mm at seat-fixing, then to Ø22mm at top of back; total length 2,140mm. Top corner inside radius R100mm. Fixing: Ø7.5mm x 50mm hexagon-head steel woodscrew; head is 5.5mm high, 13.5mm between the flats.

Backrest Steam-bent solid beech, U-shape, Ø29mm tapering to Ø22mm in the middle, ends hollowed with R12–R14.5mm to sit on backpost, held by four Ø4.5mm x 36mm domed CSK cross-headed steel woodscrews, head Ø8mm.

Stretcher ring Solid steam-bent beech, oval section, 22mm high x 20mm deep, made in three parts, finger-joints coincidental to back legs, 6.5mm pitch, 20mm height. Front corner inside radius R70mm, rear corner R100mm. Fixed with four Ø5mm x 36mm cross-headed steel woodscrews, head Ø9mm.

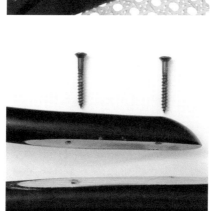

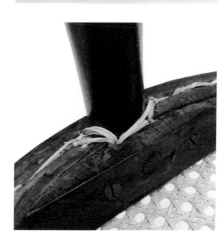

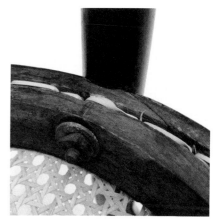

Orgone Plastic

Marc Newson 1998

⊹	Width **78** x height **83** x depth **107cm** Seating height **42–32cm**
⊿	Seat to backrest **118°** Seat to horizontal **12°**
🏋	**18.4kg**
⬈	Löffler, Germany

Marc Newson's predilection for organic forms in the 1980s and 1990s resulted in a number of formally similar pieces: the Orgone, the Orgone Stretch Lounge, the Alufelt Chair and the Event Horizon Table. Describing this family of shapes, Newson said: 'Both the interior and the exterior of the work merge together creating a fluid and utile object with a liminal space that draws the outer surface inside and vice versa: there is an interstice where the interior voids become the exterior legs. I do like the idea of creating negative space within form.'

In creating these pieces, first shown at his one-man 'Wormhole' exhibition in Milan in 1994, Newson experimented with different materials: fibreglass, wicker and aluminium. The original version of the Orgone was made in sheet aluminium by professional coachbuilders at an Aston Martin restoration workshop near London. Four years later, having gained experience of the rotation-moulding process while developing a mass-produced version of his limited-edition Bucky chair, Newson turned again to the Orgone, adapting it so it could be made in plastic.

The aim was to produce an affordable and accessible version of the chair. Only six examples of the original metal version had been made, and they are now regarded as collectors' items. In 2009 one of these six was sold for £193,000 at an auction in London – some four hundred times the price of the plastic edition.

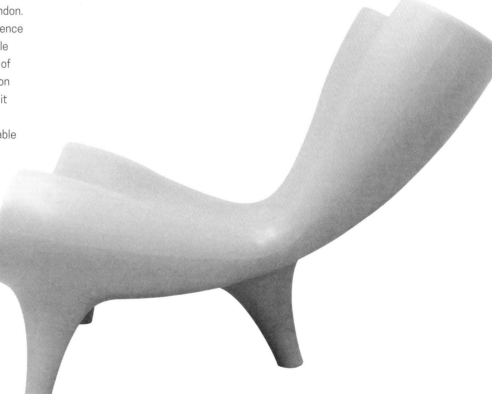

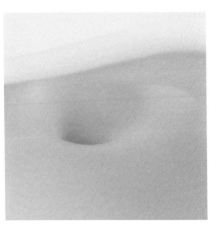
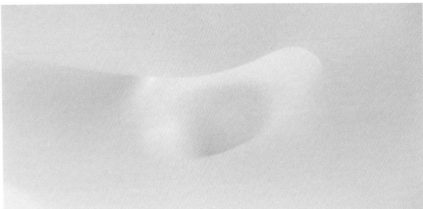

Construction

Rotational moulding in LLDPE (linear low-density polyethylene). After the moulding process, which necessarily produces a closed hollow shape, the two openings – one at each end – have to be cut out and the edges smoothed.

A key dimension of any chair is the length of the seating surface; here, it is unusually long, approx. 560mm. This underlines the more sculptural, as opposed to functional, origins of the form. Both open ends are the same width, 780mm, the overall shape being symmetric about its central bend.

Wall thickness: on average 10.5mm, varies from 9mm in the seat area to 14mm at the edge of the openings. Surface treatment: smooth, as from the metal mould. Available in various RAL colours.

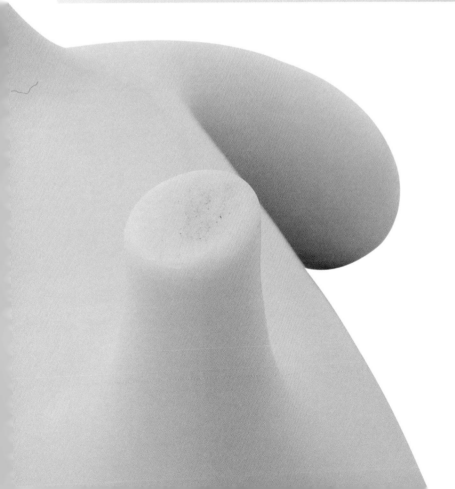

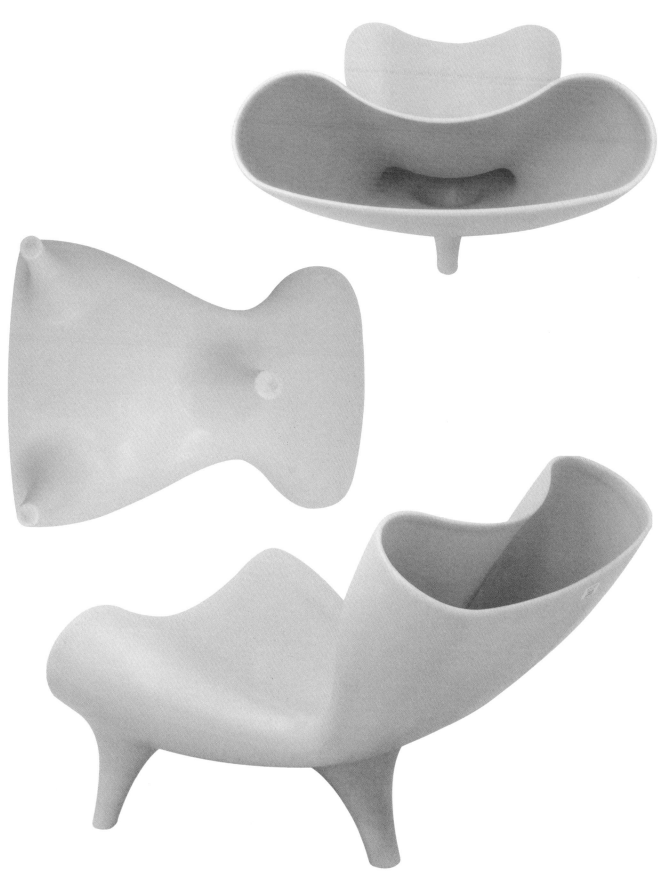

Paimio

Alvar Aalto 1931–32

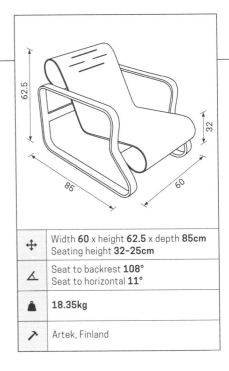

✛	Width **60** x height **62.5** x depth **85cm** Seating height **32–25cm**
∠	Seat to backrest **108°** Seat to horizontal **11°**
⚖	**18.35kg**
⚒	Artek, Finland

Created for a specific building as part of an all-encompassing design brief, the Paimio is a good example of the early use of bent plywood in chair construction. In 1929 Alvar Aalto was awarded the commission to design a sanatorium in Paimio, south-west Finland – not just the building, but also the furniture, the light fittings, the wall colours, the washbasins, even the doorknobs.

Aalto's approach to the commission was that every part of the building should support its purpose: the care of tuberculosis patients. The chair was intended for lengthy periods of sitting in the sanatorium's lecture hall, the seat being especially flexible to ease breathing. This flexibility was achieved by adding and subtracting veneer layers over the length of the plywood moulding.

The example shown here was sold by Finmar Ltd in London. As the British distributors for Artek, Finmar imported the chairs in pieces and assembled them in the UK.

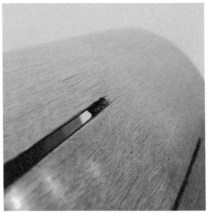

Construction

Legs and arms One continuous loop of laminated birch wood, 54.5x15mm, made up of four layers; outside two layers approx. 3mm thick, inside two approx. 4.5mm. Joined with a 4° scarf joint in the middle of the skid base over a length of approx. 210mm. Distance between armrests 492mm, leaving 8.5mm air-gap each side of the seating surface.

Seat Moulded plywood 475mm wide, fixed with glue to stretchers, and extending sideways as four tenons 69.5mm wide into mortices in the legs. The ply thickness varies over the length of the seat to provide flexibility at the appropriate places. Effectively, it is made up of three pieces: one piece starts at the top stretcher and forms the headrest roll, the backrest and the seat; another piece starts near the back of the horizontal seat and runs forward, around the roll to the bottom stretcher; a third, shorter piece starts at the bottom stretcher and runs forward and halfway round the front roll.

All three pieces were moulded together with birch veneer covering both sides in hot-metal presses. Thus, the headrest and seatback have five layers WT7mm, the seat itself seven layers WT11mm, the top half of the roll at the seat-front five layers WT7mm, the bottom half of the roll and fixing to stretcher seven layers WT11mm. The veneer layers are a combination of approx. 1mm and 2.75mm.

Curves: headrest outside R80mm, backrest to seat inside R40mm, front roll outside R80mm, all leg/armrest corner radii R80mm. Slots in headrest 3.5mm wide x 225, 220 and 125mm long.

Stretchers at top and bottom of seat: solid birch 69.5x21.5mm, rebated 5mm to engage armrest, fixing slot-headed CSK woodscrews. Rear stretcher: 59x13.5mm.

Panton Classic and PP

Verner Panton 1960

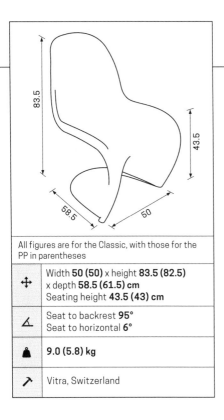

All figures are for the Classic, with those for the PP in parentheses

⛶	Width **50 (50)** x height **83.5 (82.5)** x depth **58.5 (61.5) cm** Seating height **43.5 (43) cm**
∠	Seat to backrest **95°** Seat to horizontal **6°**
🏋	**9.0 (5.8) kg**
↗	Vitra, Switzerland

When Verner Panton began experimenting with the idea of a one-piece plastic chair in 1956/57, he could not have known how long it would take to become a reality. Having made a 1:1 model of his concept in vacuum-formed polystyrene (PS) in 1960, he managed to attract the interest

of both Herman Miller and Vitra. But it wasn't until 1967, after Vitra had spent two intensive years building a total of ten prototypes, that production could begin.

The chairs were made from hand-laid fibreglass-reinforced polyester in a one-part mould. The front surface was smooth from the mould, the rear surface rougher with the texture of the glass mats (see p. 135, bottom three photos). After only 100–150 chairs had been made, production was switched to a two-part mould using Bayer's 'Baydur', a rigid polyurethane (PU) foam. While both surfaces came out smooth, the finished form needed sanding, filling and painting, adding to the production costs.

In 1971 production was changed again, this time to injection-moulded self-coloured PS. The moulding had to be thinner and of an even wall thickness, necessitating extra ribs behind the 'knee' curve and longer side-edges to provide the same strength. But both surfaces were smooth and glossy from the steel mould, so little finishing was needed. Unfortunately, the plastic (BASF's new 'Luran-S') became brittle with age and UV light. After a number of breakages, production was stopped in 1979.

Four years later the chair was reissued in PU, and in 1990 Vitra took over production, naming the chair the Panton Classic. In 1999 Vitra was able to release a polypropylene (PP) version (the right-hand chair in all comparative photos), based on the 1970s PS shape but with a varying wall thickness, obviating the need for ribs.

After thirty-plus years of development, Panton's idea for an inexpensive, one-shot, all-plastic chair had been realized, the PP version being a quarter of the price of the Classic. It is also lighter and more flexible, its surface showing a fine matt structure.

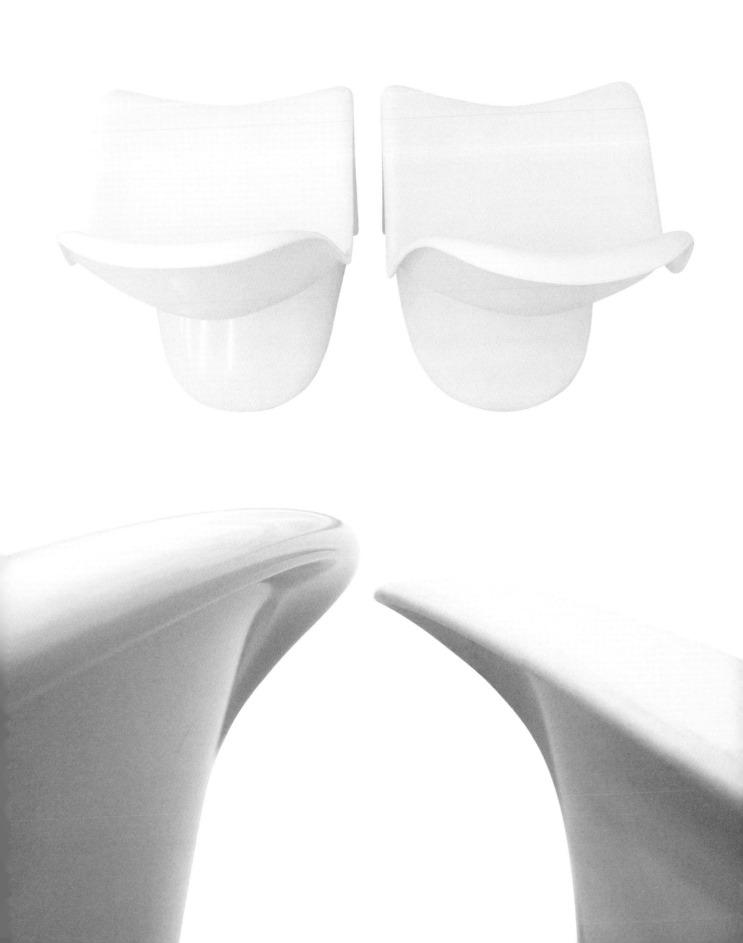

Construction

The details given below are for the Classic, with PP values in parentheses.

Body One-piece rigid PU foam moulding, trimmed, sanded, fillered, high-gloss lacquer (PP: injection moulding, self-coloured). Wall thicknesses: back top edge 10.5mm (4.5mm), back centre 12mm (4.5mm), back/seat curve 13.5mm (6mm), seat centre 15.5mm (7mm), centre 25mm (8mm), seat/skirt curve-edges 30mm (19mm), skirt sides centre 14.5mm (5.5mm), skirt front edge 17mm (8mm), skirt bottom centre 18mm (5mm). Radii: back/seat curve approx. R75mm (R65mm), seat/skirt curve approx. R45mm (R50mm).

Feet Raised section at front of skirt 88mm long, then 2.2mm rebate for 270mm before raised again for back foot around centre section of skirt (PP: no feet).

In 2008 Vitra reintroduced the children's version in PP, the Panton Junior, width 365mm, height 605mm, depth 480mm, seating height 320mm.

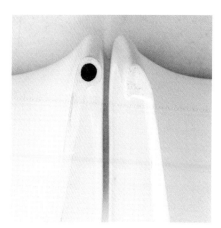

PAW

Charles and Ray Eames 1948

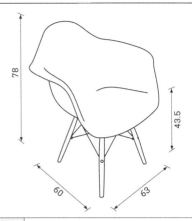

⊹	Width **63** x height **78** x depth **60cm** Seating height **43.5cm**
⊿	Seat to back **100°** Seat to horizontal **10°**
⬛	**5.35kg**
↗	Zenith Plastics for Herman Miller, USA (until c. 1958)

The arms of the PAW (Pivoting Arm Wood) illustrated here display a rare detail: the rope-edge, a feature specified by the Eameses to soften the outside edge of the GRP (glass-filled reinforced plastic) shell (see photo p. 138, top right). Inspired by the rolled edges of the bumpers on a Ford Model T, they had already experimented with a similar finish on their pressed-metal shells, using a McGee-Wirer to flange the edges over a steel wire. Unfortunately, the rope-edge added to the overall cost of the PAW, and was soon dropped from production.

The swivel unit was a standard item produced by the Seng Company of Chicago, an established supplier of furniture fittings. On p. 138, one can see how adapter brackets had to be used between shell and swivel, not only to adjust the height, but also to connect the asymmetrically placed shock mounts to the symmetrical shape of the swivel plate.

For more on the history of the chair, see p. 80 and the description of the Eameses' DSW chair.

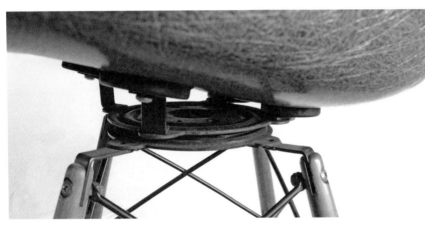

Construction

Seat shell GRP (using 50.8mm/
2 in. chopped strands of fibreglass),
WT3.5–4mm, rising to 4.5mm in corners,
reinforced with twisted fibreglass rope
Ø4.8mm (³⁄₁₆ in.) moulded into the edge,
forming a radius of approx. R3mm on the
outside edge.

Base fixing Four rubber shock mounts
Ø63.3mm (2½ in.) x 10mm thick, bonded
with epoxy glue, each with embedded
steel discs threaded M6 to take cross-
headed screws to fix four steel brackets
19mm wide, WT3mm. Front and rear
brackets are different heights to fit the
curve of the shell. These connect to two
circular swivel plates: Ø170mm, WT3mm,
each with a circular pressed groove (ball-
race) containing five Ø10mm steel balls.
Bottom swivel plate is spot-welded to two
steel strips 19mm x WT3mm, which cross
each other and are bent down at each end
to engage the four legs. Additional seam
welding is used between the strips and
disc at the outside edge.

Legs Turned beech 365mm long, tapering
from Ø19.5mm at the foot to Ø26mm at
the middle fixing, then to Ø20mm at the
top fixing. The version shown here was
made before the internal steel reinforcing
rods in the legs and the steel collars for
the fixing screws were introduced (see
DSW chair, p. 82). Leg triangulation:
Ø6.4mm (¼ in.) steel rods, four V-shaped
elements welded into one unit, corners
flattened and drilled for 6mm. Leg-fixing
screws: Ø6mm cross-headed, Ø14.5mm
head, self-locking 10mm hexagon nuts
with nylon insert.

Feet Ø18mm x 4mm polypropylene, fixed
with embedded pin or screw.

Pelt

Benjamin Hubert   2012

This deceptively simple chair combines traditional cabinet-making expertise with the latest technology. It is therefore a prime example of a modern approach to chair design, embracing digitalization in the context of traditional craft skills.

Such an approach becomes clear when one examines the joints between the frame and the rear legs, where the wood has been machined to twist visually and present the tenon in the right place. At first glance this is a relatively straightforward joint, but the geometry is in fact quite complex, solved by using CAD for the construction and CNC milling machines to cut the wood (see line drawing, p. 142).

Sadly, despite successful prototyping by the Italian company De La Espada, the chair has yet to be put into full production.

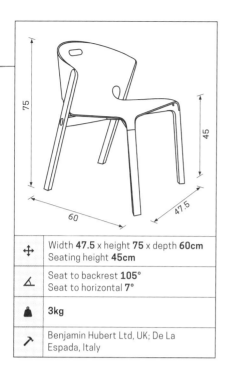

✛	Width **47.5** x height **75** x depth **60cm** Seating height **45cm**
◿	Seat to backrest **105°** Seat to horizontal **7°**
🏋	**3kg**
⟋	Benjamin Hubert Ltd, UK; De La Espada, Italy

Construction

Shell Five-layer birch plywood veneered both sides with ash (seven layers in total), WT 7.5mm. Pierced at top of backrest with a slot hole 100x30mm as a carrying handle. Shell is fixed to the frame and legs with glue.

Front legs Solid ash rectangular section 35x25mm, joined to the cross frame with an open mortice and tenon 35x15mm, secured with a Ø10mm dowel (see line drawing, below). Top of the leg rebated at front 7.5mm to accept the ply seat, radius leg/seat approx. R50mm.

Rear legs Solid ash rectangular section 35x25mm, rebated 7.5mm to accept the backrest, section then tapering to 35x10mm at the top. Top end half-round R17.5mm. Legs joined to cross frame with rounded-through mortice and tenon 35x15mm, visibly wedged from outside. All legs finished at the bottom with nylon skid feet.

Seating frame Two solid-ash rails in cross form, rectangular section 35x50mm, central cross-lap joint glued. Tenon at rear end with horizintal kerf to accept wedge. An earlier version used a central screw for the frame, and a dowel through the rear leg joint (see photo left). As the rear legs are tipped forward at approx 70°, and the rails are set at approx. 45°, the back half of the rail has to be machined to give it a slight twist, and the tenon angled in two dimensions to fit into the leg mortice.

Pressed

Harry Thaler 2010

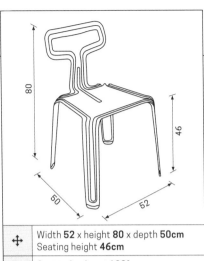

⊕	Width **52** x height **80** x depth **50cm** Seating height **46cm**
∡	Seat to backrest **103°** Seat to horizontal **2.8°** (centre **10.2°**)
⚖	**2.75kg**
⚒	Nils Holger Moormann, Germany

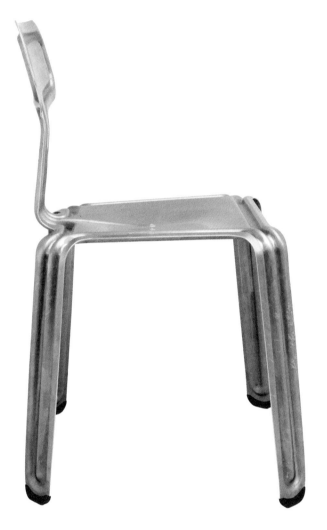

With Pressed, Harry Thaler succeeded in realizing the goal of many designers over the decades: a chair made of one piece of material, given form by means of one production process (see also DSW, p. 80; Panton, p. 132; Zig Zag, p. 224). Indeed, he attained this holy grail of chair design in a very simple way, using the properties of the material and process to produce a stable, even stackable chair. Of particular note is the transformation of a flexible material – aluminium – to a stiff, load-bearing one through folding and pressing or swaging.

Pressed was Thaler's final project for his master's degree at the Royal College of Art. The prototype had one continuous groove running around the perimeter, and was cut from a single square metre of metal. The extra central groove in the middle of the backrest post, the separate plastic clip-on feet (attached with a hidden fixing detail) and the drainage hole in the seat were added later.

After graduating, Thaler developed the prototype through to production in conjunction with the German furniture entrepreneur Nils Holger Moormann. A further development was the creation of a matching stool made out of the scrap pieces of aluminium left over after cutting out the chair blank from a larger sheet. The stool is formed from three identical parts – each comprising a leg with a 120° seat section – which are cut out, pressed and then screwed together.

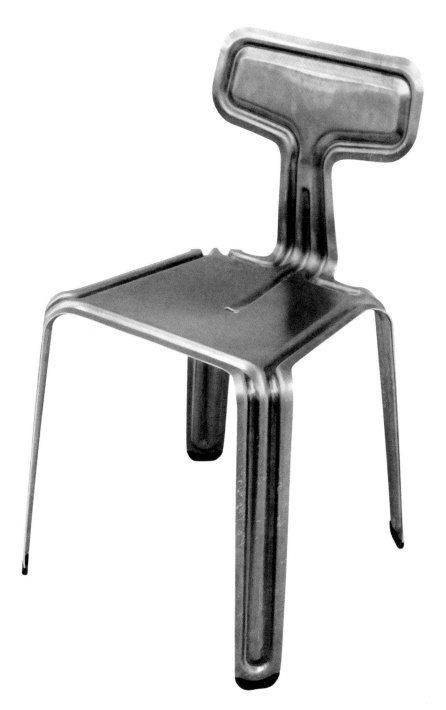

Construction

Chair body Laser-cut out of aluminium sheet, WT2.5mm, diagonal dimension before bending back foot to front foot 1,415mm. All grooves have inside radius R6mm. Continuous outside and central grooves pressed while flat, then backrest and legs bent and pressed into position.

Backrest post 100mm wide at top tapering to 125mm at bottom. Seat/backrest-post angle 80.6°, with radius R25mm; at top of backrest post, angle tips backwards giving seat/backrest 103°. Top outside corners of backrest radii R50mm, backrest/slat inside radii R25mm. Seat/leg radii R35mm at edge, at centre ridge R25mm. Seat pierced with one drainage hole for rain, Ø9mm x 24.8mm.

Legs 81mm wide at seat tapering down to 72.5mm at foot. Front leg/floor angle 96.5°, back leg/floor angle 77.5°, bottom edge of leg (which sits in plastic foot) angled inwards 10° to stand nearer vertical. Bottom edge radius R45mm, with undercut shoulders at 57.5mm width to grip foot. Central keyhole-shaped cutout, Ø4.5mm hole 7.5mm from outside edge, opened with V-slot 4.5–3.1mm.

Feet TPE moulding 70mm long x 13mm high in centre, width at top 5mm, at bottom 10mm. Inside face slope 13°, bottom corner radii R25mm. Slot 2.5mm wide, 58mm long, interrupted by 4mm bridge to engage keyhole-slot in leg.

The chair is also available with a powder coating in various colours.

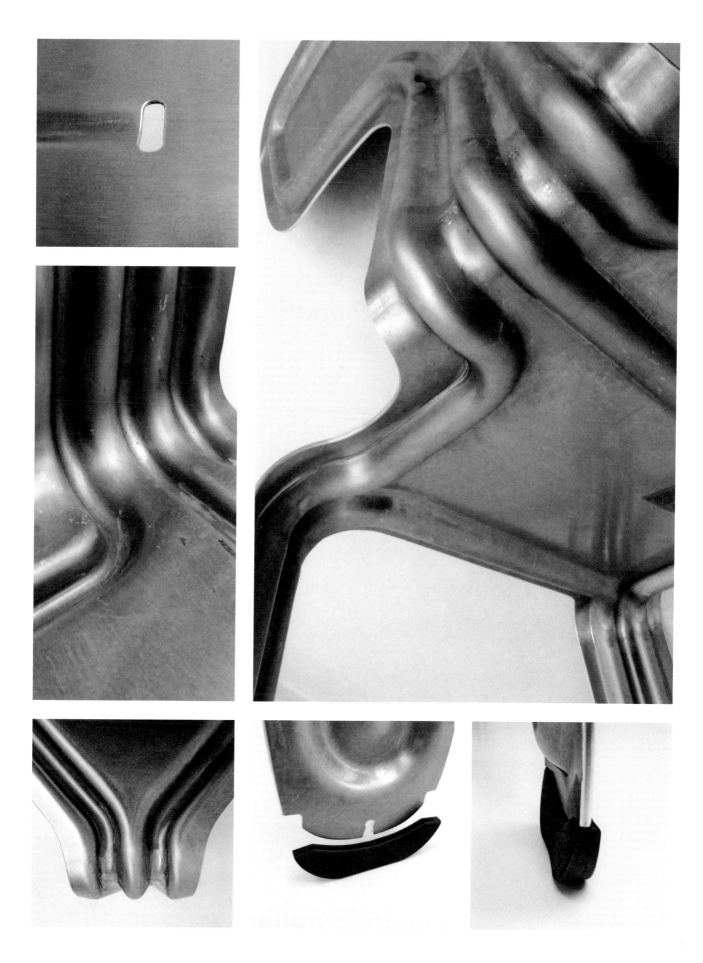

Red-Blue

Gerrit Rietveld 1918

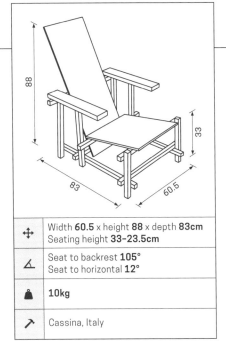

⊕	Width **60.5** x height **88** x depth **83cm** Seating height **33–23.5cm**
⊿	Seat to backrest **105°** Seat to horizontal **12°**
⚖	**10kg**
↗	Cassina, Italy

Gerrit Rietveld's Red-Blue chair marks a turning point in furniture design. Reacting to the heavy upholstered furniture of the nineteenth century, Rietveld devised a chair based purely on lines and surfaces. Seven years before Marcel Breuer's B3/Wassily chair, Rietveld produced a light, open construction, in which the form and the concept dominated, not the material or the comfort.

Originally, the chair was produced in a plain, stained-wood finish, or in just a single colour – white, pink, green or black. It was not until 1923 that the now famous red-blue version was made available. The chair was seen as an abstract-realistic sculpture, a physical manifesto for De Stijl, the circle of Dutch abstract artists of which Rietveld was a member.

The geometric, constructivist aesthetic of standardized elements was subject to many small variations over the years. Early versions often had rectangular side panels fixed to the inside of the vertical posts. A white model from the early 1920s features irregular side panels, with the bottom edge running parallel to the seat.

Construction

Seat 12.5mm plywood, 400mm wide x 460mm deep, painted dark blue, fixed to the frame using M5 x 35mm socket-head CSK machine screws, head Ø9.5mm, 3mm socket key. Screws fix through the frame into four M5 brass double-threaded inserts in the bottom side.

Backrest 12.5mm plywood, 345mm wide x 900mm long, painted red, fixed to the frame with 3x20mm steel L-brackets drilled Ø4mm and countersunk, using Ø4mm x 16mm cross-headed CSK woodscrews.

Earlier versions show various different fixing methods for the seat and backrest. An unpainted 1919 version has the backrest held by horizontal dowels approx. Ø12mm; a 1921 version uses nails roughly covered with filler before painting (see photo this page, top left).

Frame and legs Square-section beech, 30x30mm, joined at right-angles using one Ø10mm beech dowel per join (Rietveld's original drawings show dowels Ø16mm x 45mm long). Where three parts are joined, i.e. leg, rail and stretcher, two of the three dowels sit in blind holes and are not visible; the third dowel, which must be fitted from the outside using a through hole, is visible, and is therefore arranged to point downwards (see photo this page, top right).

Armrests Beech, 455x85x30mm, each fixed to the rear stretcher with two Ø10mm vertical beech dowels, and halfway along to the forward post with a mortice and tenon joint. The rounded-end tenon on the post approx. 12mm wide x 25mm long x 25mm high, aligned to the length of the armrest. Height of armrest from floor: 500mm.

Round

Hans J. Wegner 1949

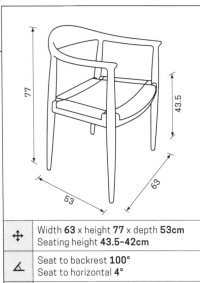

⊹	Width **63** x height **77** x depth **53cm** Seating height **43.5–42cm**
◿	Seat to backrest **100°** Seat to horizontal **4°**
⚖	**4.85kg**
⌁	PP Møbler, Denmark

With the Round chair, Hans Wegner succeeded in realizing his desire to combine a knowledge of and respect for traditional Danish craftsmanship with the aesthetics of the early modern Scandinavian design movement. Its successful release in the United States in 1950 marked Wegner's international breakthrough as a furniture designer. In fact, so great was its impact in America that in 1960, when John F. Kennedy and Richard Nixon met in the first-ever, televised presidential election debate, the seat chosen for the occasion was an upholstered version of the Round, which was thereafter known in the US simply as 'the Chair'.

The version shown here is a historic example with a wicker seat, made by Johannes Hansen in 1949. Since 1990 the chairs have been produced by PP Møbler (under the names pp501 and pp503, for the wicker and upholstered versions respectively) using wood from two-hundred-year-old trees. The rough shapes for the back and armrests are cut from freshly sawn planks, and then conditioned for at least another two years. The right and left armrests are cut parallel to each other out of one plank and paired to match; they are then shaped to the final form by hand.

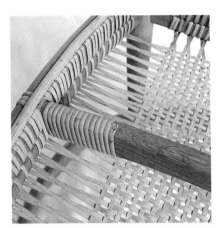

Construction

The four photos opposite, top left, which show production of the pp501 and pp531, were all taken in the PP Møbler workshops.

Seating surface Woven cane from the Indonesian rattan vine, additionally fixed to bottom of stretchers with a half-round strip of cane approx. 9mm wide, nailed into position. The version with an upholstered leather seat is known as the pp503, and was designed in 1950.

Backrest and arms Sawn and shaped oak, three parts joined using wedged-tenon finger-joints. Backrest 113x26mm in the centre, tapering and flattening towards the arms. Arms 76x27mm at the widest point.

Legs Solid turned oak. Rear leg Ø41mm at seat height, tapering to Ø28mm at the junction with armrest, Ø24mm at the foot. Front leg Ø41mm at seat, tapering to Ø28mm at the junction with armrest, Ø24mm at the foot. Legs joined to the seat stretchers with mortise and tenon, to backrest and arms with an approx. Ø12mm peg turned on the top of the legs.

Stretchers Side stretchers 64x25mm section, half-round at top and bottom, with a 3mm horizontal slot between the sides and along the bottom edge, to take the rattan. Front and rear stretchers 60x26mm section, half-round at top and bottom, also with a 3mm slot between the sides and on the bottom. Front stretcher bows 20mm forwards, dropping 20mm at the centre. Rear stretcher bows 25mm backwards, dropping 10mm at the centre. Central stretcher 36x17mm section, dropping approx. 45mm in a flat curve towards the middle (the pp503 has no central stretcher).

The chair is available in oak, ash or cherry, and with various surface treatments: soaped or oiled (oak, ash), or lacquered (oak, ash, cherry).

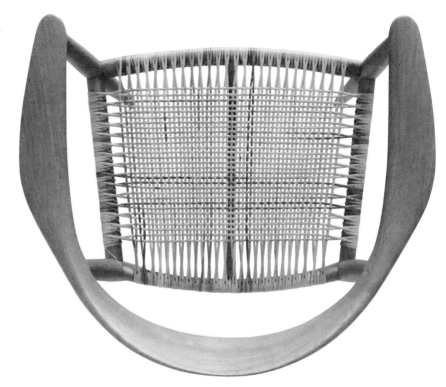

S 33/S 34

Mart Stam 1926

Mart Stam first presented his idea for a metal cantilever chair in 1926 at a preparatory meeting for the Weissenhof architectural exhibition in Stuttgart, a residential development built to showcase modernist housing. Stam's new idea was noticed by the architects Mies van der Rohe and Heinz and Bodo Rasch, all of whom, one year later, employed the cantilever form in designs of their own: the MR 10 (Mies) and the Sitzgeiststuhl (the Rasch brothers). The MR 10 was shown at the Weissenhof exhibition alongside Stam's S 33, and both were seen by Marcel Breuer, who subsequently produced his own cantilever chair, initially called the B32 but later renamed the Cesca or S 32 (see p. 52).

To build his prototype, Stam used gas piping, the narrow corner radii being achieved with standard cast corner-pieces. For the exhibition chairs, the furniture manufacturer Arnold used hot-bent iron tubing to avoid the visible cast joints. This tubing proved too soft to take loads, and had to be reinforced with a solid iron core, resulting in a stable but rigid construction. In contrast, Mies's MR 10, with its large radii made of cold-formed seamless steel tubing, was flexible and provided greater comfort.

When Thonet took over production of the S 33, it used standard steel tubing with slightly larger corner radii. In the S 34 version, the front legs rise above the seat to form arms and then the support for the backrest, the seat and backrest being secured by two L-shaped pieces. The historic chairs shown here are not the current licensed versions from Thonet.

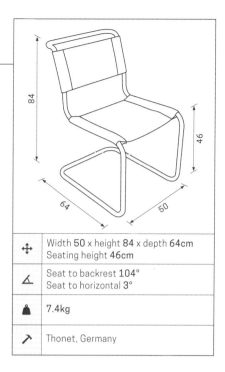

✛	Width **50** x height **84** x depth **64**cm Seating height **46**cm
◿	Seat to backrest **104°** Seat to horizontal **3°**
⚖	7.4kg
⚒	Thonet, Germany

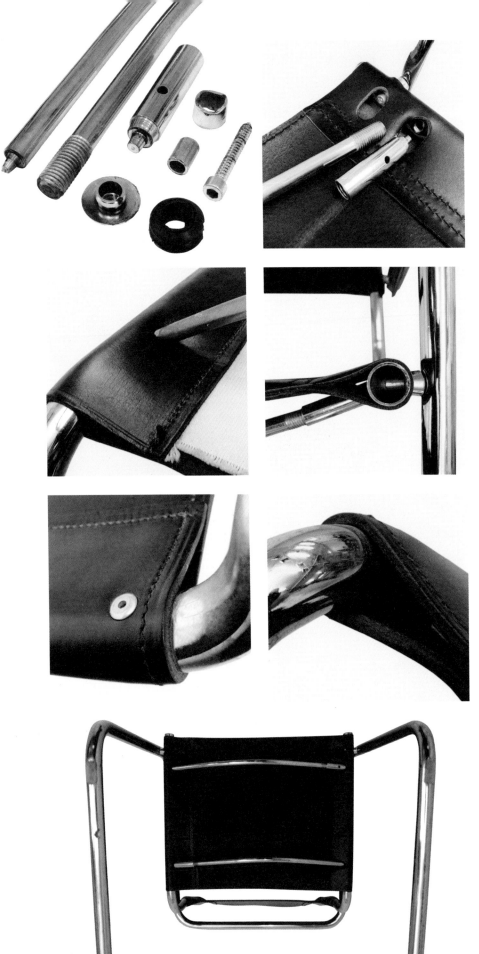

Construction

Frame Chromed steel tubing Ø25mm, WT2mm, all corners inside radii R60mm. Seating rails drilled with four Ø8mm holes to take two chromed-steel tensioning rods (stretchers) Ø12mm, curved in an arc of R325mm, threaded at one end M12 x 1.75mm. On this end sits a steel tensioning piece Ø18mm x 77.5mm, drilled through with Ø6mm to assist turning (using a screwdriver or similar), threaded M12 x 1.75mm, chamfered at the end to Ø13.5mm, ending with a Ø7.4–6.4mm x 7mm cone. The other end of each tensioning rod also has a Ø7.4–6.4mm x 7mm cone to engage the seat rail.

S 34 version (with arms): each seat rail/backpost fixed to leg/armrest with two Ø6mm x 51.5mm socket-head self-tapping screws, head 6mm high, positioned with a steel spacer tube Ø10mm x 14.7mm, WT1mm, inside the seat rail (to keep screw-head accessible). Between rail and leg the screw passes through a steel spacer tube Ø16mm x 12mm, WT1.5mm, shaped both ends with R12.5mm to match the leg and seat rail; same applies between leg and backpost (see photos this page, second column, second from top, and opposite). Seat rail drilled inside Ø10mm to take spacer and outside Ø7mm for fixing screws. Also drilled four x Ø8mm to take stretchers. Tubes closed at both ends with Ø25mm chromed PS stopper, 1mm at edge, dome rising to 3.5mm. Rear centre tube Ø11.7mm, WT1mm, with one Ø12.7mm ring, sitting in a black polypropylene ringed plug Ø15mm, WT1.5mm, two tapered rings 2.3mm thick, Ø22mm.

Leather 3.5mm thick full-grain butt leather. On S 33, backrest held in position with two Ø9.5mm aluminium pop-rivets to stop the leather slipping down the backposts.

Safari

Kaare Klint 1933

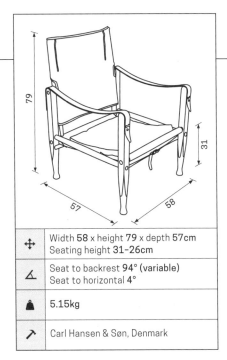

⊹	Width **58** x height **79** x depth **57**cm Seating height **31–26cm**
⊿	Seat to backrest **94°** (variable) Seat to horizontal **4°**
🏋	5.15kg
⚒	Carl Hansen & Søn, Denmark

Kaare Klint's inspiration for this portable chair was a photograph in the 1928 book *Safari: A Saga of the African Blue*, in which the American husband-and-wife explorers and film-makers Martin and Osa Johnson recall their three-year travels in Africa. Pictured in the photo – a scene featuring one of the Johnsons' camps; see p. 96 of the fifteenth edition – was a version of the Roorkhee chair, named after the British headquarters of the Indian Army Corps of Engineers in India, where this type of mobile chair had been developed for the military towards the end of the nineteenth century. Klint was attracted to the simplicity and honesty of the chair's design: each part is fit for purpose, there are no superfluous elements, it can be put together without glue, and the joints tighten up when loaded.

Owing to the flexible nature of its construction, the Safari can cope with uneven surfaces, is very light, and can be packed up in minutes and transported in a canvas bag approximately 24cm in diameter and 60cm long. The green example shown here is a historic version built by Rud Rasmussen in the 1960s.

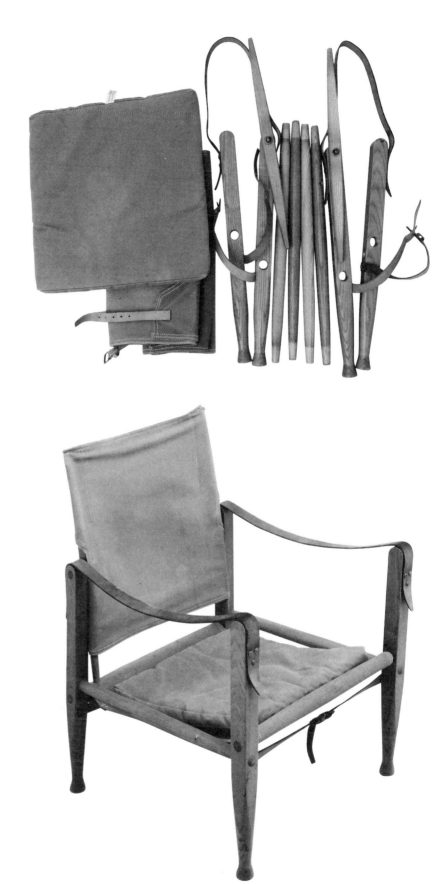

Construction

Legs Solid ash, square section 40x40mm, 553mm long, lower section turned and tapered to Ø27mm, then out to foot Ø38mm, drilled with tapered hole Ø24–20mm to accept side and rear stretchers. Rear legs also drilled with a stepped hole Ø19mm x 5.5mm deep, continuing Ø8mm to hold backrest bolt, centred on R22mm top radius. Front, side and rear stretchers solid ash tapered from Ø33mm in the middle to Ø20mm at ends, 570mm long.

Backrest side rails Solid turned ash Ø32mm in the middle, tapering to Ø16mm at ends, flattened both sides to 14mm thickness, 520mm long (see photo this page, top left). Fixed with a brass, disc-headed BSW ⁵⁄₃₂ in. (4mm) bolt; disc is Ø ¾ in. x ³⁄₁₆ in. (Ø19mm x 4.8mm) without a slot (see photo opposite). Bolt held with a brass, domed cap-nut ¹⁹⁄₃₂ in. (15.1mm) high, ⁹⁄₁₆ in. (14.3mm) between flats; the cap-nut in turn is locked with a BSW ⁵⁄₁₆ in. (7.9mm) slotted grub screw. Brass washers under nut and between the rail and backpost are Ø ¾ in. x ³⁄₃₂ in. (Ø19mm x 2.4mm; see photo this page, top left). The rails are impressed on one side with the word 'Denmark'.

Armrests Saddle leather 35mm wide, 3.5mm thick, fixed each end with three 3x25mm brass CSK slotted woodscrews sitting in Ø10mm brass countersunk rosettes.

Tensioning straps between legs Saddle leather 20mm wide, 3mm thick, fixed by two screws as above.

Seat, backrest and cushion 100% linen canvas, makers label 'Rud Rasmussens Snedkerier, Copenhagen N, Denmark'.

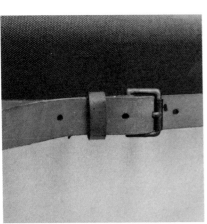

Sedia 1 (1123 xP)

Enzo Mari 1974

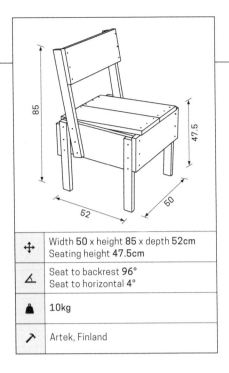

✛	Width **50** x height **85** x depth **52cm** Seating height **47.5cm**
∡	Seat to backrest **96°** Seat to horizontal **4°**
🏋	10kg
⚒	Artek, Finland

While it may look like a simple, inexpensive design for a DIY chair, the Sedia 1 is in fact the expression of a sociopolitical approach to furniture design and manufacture. In 1974, at the Galleria Milano in Italy, Enzo Mari presented a range of wooden furniture – the Sedia 1 included – made exclusively out of sawn planks and nails. The plans for each item of furniture were collected together in a book, *Proposta per un'autoprogettazione* (Proposal for a Self-Design), and visitors were encouraged to use these plans to make the furniture themselves.

Mari's idea was that by building the objects with their own hands, out of planks and nails, people would come to understand the thinking behind them. They would learn the principles of furniture-making, and would thereby be able to critique the values involved in mass production, specifically the issue of quantity vs quality. According to Mari, 'the quality is determined when the shape of a product does not "seem" but simply "is".'

In his foreword to the 2002 reissue of *Autoprogettazione*, Mari reiterated the educational value of the project. Artek began offering the chair as a kit of sawn parts in 2012; the chair shown here, however, was made by the author himself, from scratch, using the plans in *Autoprogettazione*.

Sedia 1 (1123 xP)

 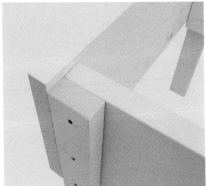 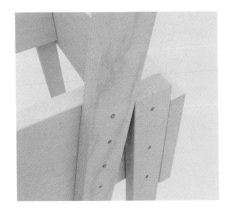

Construction

All parts untreated spruce.

Legs Four 50x25x440mm.

Stiles (back posts) Two 50x25x610mm.

Seat Two 200x25x520mm.

Backrest and front/rear rails
Three 200x25x500mm.

Side rails Two 200x25x470mm.

Fixings Fifty-two steel nails
Ø2.5mm x 45mm.

The front rail sits 10mm above the top of the front leg, the rear rail 25mm below the top of the back leg. In this way the seat is fixed at the ergonomically comfortable angle of 4°.

To ensure the correct angle of each stile, the top rear corner of the stile should be in line with the back of the rear rail, the back side of the stile should touch the top corner of the rear leg, and the bottom corner of the stile should coincide with the bottom edge of the side rail. This is easier to achieve than it sounds: by laying the chair on its back, the correct position of each stile can be marked out before the nails are driven in.

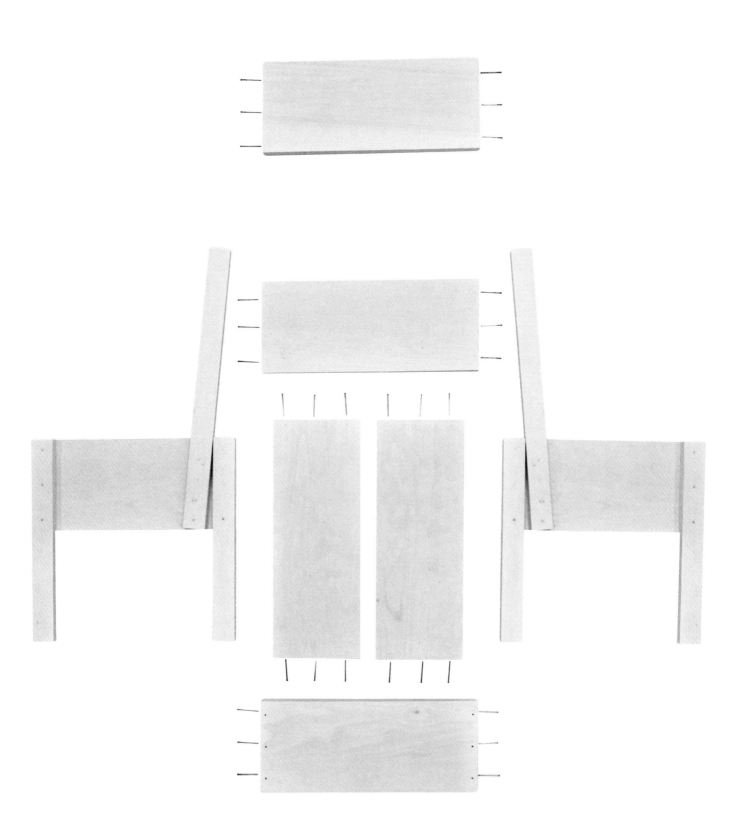

Seggiolina Pop

Enzo Mari 2004

The Seggiolina Pop is a good example of technology transfer. Through the addition of a structural 'skeleton', Enzo Mari was able to give a material originally intended for use in the car industry – expanded polypropylene, or EPP – a novel application: children's furniture.

EPP is a relatively new material, developed in Japan by JSP towards the end of the 1970s and first applied as an energy absorber in car bumpers in 1982. Since then, it has also been used in packaging, insulation and flotation devices. The manufacturing process uses steam and pressure to expand beads of PP within a metal mould, the combination of heat and pressure causing the beads to expand and bond together (sintering).

The surface of the chair displays small circular groups of bumps. These are the impressions left by the tiny holes that allow the steam to escape from the mould during the expanding process (see photos at top of p. 171).

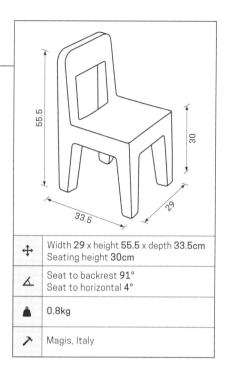

✛	Width **29** x height **55.5** x depth **33.5cm** Seating height **30cm**
∡	Seat to backrest **91°** Seat to horizontal **4°**
⬤	0.8kg
↗	Magis, Italy

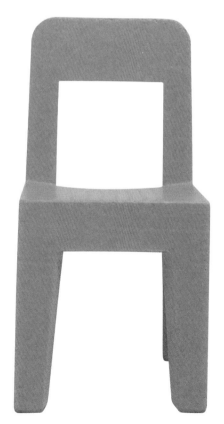

Seggiolina Pop

Construction

As EPP is stronger in compression than in tension, Mari has embedded two H-shaped high-density PP supporting frames within the sides of the chair to take up the sideways forces. During the expansion process, the frames are held in position inside the steam chest (mould) by a series of clips. The space taken up by each of these clips can be observed on the underside of the seat (see photo opposite, top left): the four holes reveal the points at which the frame was held by the clips. On the frame itself, small dimples show where the clips were located (see photo this page, second column, second from bottom), the edge-strengthening ribs being interrupted at this point for the clips to withdraw downwards out of the mould after the expanding process.

Body Expanded PP, seat 40mm thick, reinforced underneath by ribs 33mm wide, 9.5° draft angle. Holes for positioning clips 11x12mm.

Frame Two identical parts, black high-density PP, leg section 35mm wide, WT4mm, with strengthening edges 4mm high forming a flattened H-section, WT4mm, width tapering down to flat section 12mm wide at bottom of leg. Smaller stiffening ribs WT3.5mm, 3mm high. Backrest support 34.5mm wide at seat height, tapering as a T-section to 11.5mm wide x 15mm deep at the top. At the junction of seat and backrest support, the frame has an open three-quarter ring Ø9.6mm to facilitate the flexing of backrest.

Standard

Jean Prouvé 1934–50

Designed in 1950 by Jean Prouvé for the cafeteria of the Conservatoire National des Arts et Métiers in Paris, the Standard chair (also known as No. 305) is the final reworking of an earlier design by Prouvé from 1934, the No. 4. Between 1941 and 1951, Prouvé also produced two demountable versions: the No. 300 (pictured in red on p. 175), and, as a result of war-related metal rationing, the all-wooden No. 301 (not illustrated).

The metal versions of the chair – the No. 300 and the Standard – are notable for Prouvé's use of both sheet and tubular metal in the frame. The rear legs are fabricated from sheet steel (the welding joints are along the two forward edges), the strength of the triangular form taking up the greater forces caused by users tipping the chair backwards.

A cunning constructional detail of the Standard (visible only with an endoscope; see photo p. 174, centre right) is the second point at which the side rail is attached to the rear leg – a small plug welded to the inside face of the leg. This provides the necessary strength that the visible weld alone (where the rail enters the leg) would not have given.

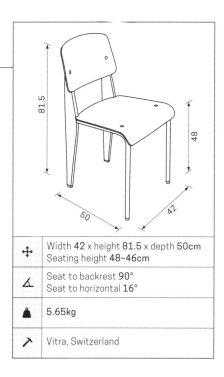

⊹	Width **42** x height **81.5** x depth **50cm** Seating height **48–46cm**
⊿	Seat to backrest **90°** Seat to horizontal **16°**
🏋	5.65kg
🛠	Vitra, Switzerland

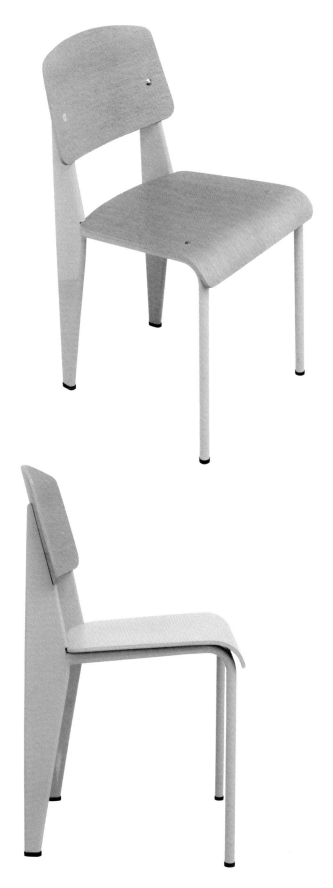

Construction

Seating surface Seven-layer plywood, WT8mm, fixed with two drilled-spanner cap-headed nuts sitting on M5 threaded rods welded on to the frame bracket; bracket 30mm wide x 32mm long, half-round, WT3mm, welded to the side rail. Plywood drilled Ø8.5mm with a Ø15.5mm x 3mm sink for the cap-nut. Rear edge of seat held in two 9.5mm cut-outs, one in each back leg (see photo opposite, first column, centre), then tensioned down on to two Ø15mm clear silicon stoppers on the side rail by the front fixing nuts. (The demountable No. 300 uses two flat metal strips to hold the seat – see photo this page, top right – a more expensive solution than the cut-outs on the legs of the Standard.) Cap-nuts with stepped head, Ø18mm very flat dome to 0.5mm edge (two Ø1.5mm spanner holes at 8.5mm distance), then Ø15mm x 1.5mm, shaft Ø8mm x 10mm, internal thread M5.

Backrest Plywood, same as seat. Cap-nuts engage the threaded rod attached to a steel insert welded into the cut-out in the back leg.

Back leg 1.4mm sheet steel in elongated-hole section, tapering from 18x36mm at foot to 18x96mm at seat. Welding seam on front (sloping) edge.

Front leg Steel tube Ø22.2mm (⅞ in.), WT1.5mm, tapered after seat bracket by horizontal crushing down to 15mm wide x 27.3mm high to fit inside rear leg, where it is fixed to the inside wall with a welded plug (see photo opposite, centre right).

Front and rear stretcher Steel tube Ø22.2mm, WT1.5mm.

Feet Black PP mouldings. Front: Ø24.5mm x 9mm, push-fitted over bottom of leg tube. Rear: Ø20.7mm x 38.5mm, 9mm visible, push-fitted 21mm high within leg.

Surface treatment Metal: powder-coated; oak veneer: clear matt varnish.

Steelwood

Ronan and Erwan Bouroullec 2007

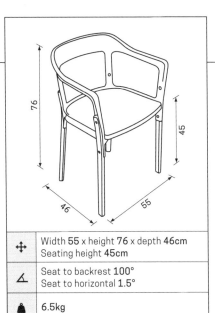

⊹	Width **55** x height **76** x depth **46cm** Seating height **45cm**
⊿	Seat to backrest 100° Seat to horizontal 1.5°
⚖	6.5kg
⚒	Magis, Italy

The Bouroullecs' original commission for the Steelwood was to design an inexpensive wooden chair, using small pressed-steel parts to join together larger wooden elements. Eugenio Perazza, owner of Magis, arranged for the brothers to visit a metal-stamping works in northern Italy, where they discovered the possibilities offered by automated metal-working. They thus decided to increase the proportion of steel in the design, concentrating the complexity of the manufacturing processes in the steel elements, rather than in the traditionally hand-made wooden parts. The resulting design combines the backrest, armrests and leg fixings in a single, apparently simple metal form that belies the advanced technology and high level of automation involved.

The chair is almost entirely machine made; only the surface finishing of the wood and the final assembly are done by hand. The steel frame is pressed from flat sheet, the complexity of the form requiring nine separate pressing, stamping and welding operations. Interestingly, the angle of the backrest requires the rear legs to have a slightly different form from those at the front, evidence that the designers did not sacrifice the aesthetics or comfort of their design to the rationality of using four identical legs.

The Steelwood collection includes bar stools, tables and shelving units, all employing the two-material design.

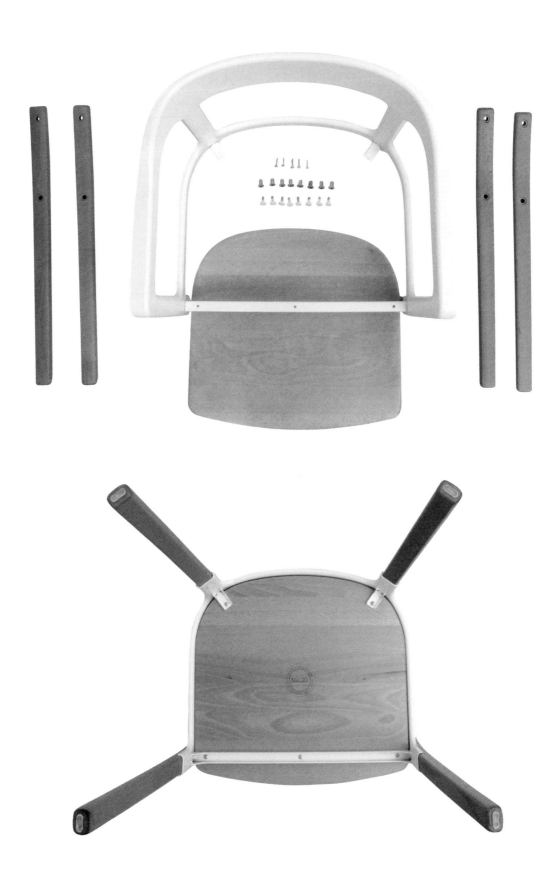

Steelwood

Construction

Backrest and frame One-piece pressed 355MC steel (see glossary), chosen for its good cold-forming characteristics, WT 2mm; front stretcher and rear brackets folded steel, WT 2mm.

Starting with a flat sheet of metal, the central window and screw holes are sheared and punched out, then the edges coined and trimmed. After folding around the sides, the side windows are sheared out and coined, then the sides slightly curved, i.e. twisted to open up the space between the armrests. Finally, the front stretcher and rear brackets are welded on to the frame.

Seat Solid beech 25mm thick, fixed to the brackets and stretcher with five Ø3.5mm cross-headed screws. Wooden seating surface milled out max. 5mm deep to form an ergonomic shape.

Legs CNC-machined solid beech 34.5x31mm, tapering between lower fixing and foot down to 31x21mm. The front and back legs are not identical; the top curve of the front legs is flatter. Legs drilled twice Ø10mm, with Ø15mm x 2mm sinks on the outside surface to take the cap-nuts, and two Ø18mm x 3mm sinks on the inside for the coach-bolt recess. Leg fixing: two M6 coach-bolts with Ø15mm flat heads, which screw into socket-head cap-nuts Ø9mm.

Feet Moulded polypropylene 20x8mm, rounded ends R4mm, WT 4mm, with ribbed shaft 10mm high x 15mm long, WT 3mm, push-fitted in milled hole. The 4mm top of the foot sits in the 2mm-deep rebate to reduce wear and improve resilience.

Surface treatment Steel: powder-coated in white, black or red, or galvanized. Wood: semi-matt laquer in transparent, white, black or red.

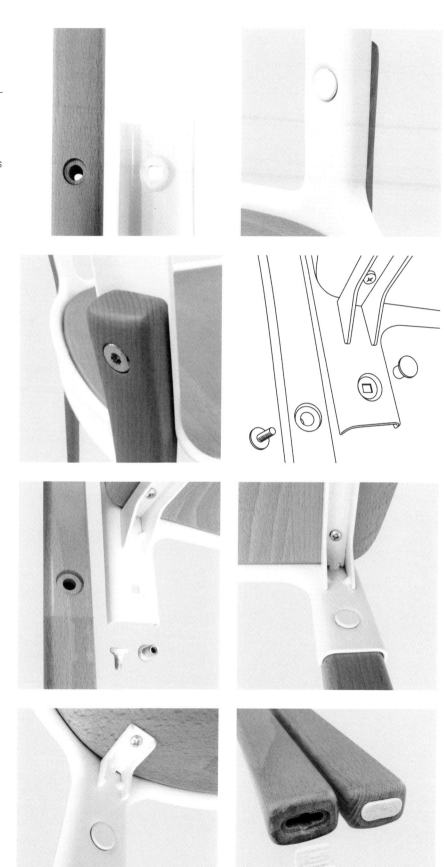

Stool One

Konstantin Grcic 2006

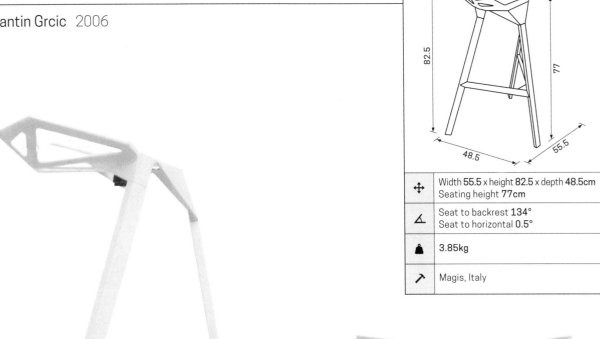

✛	Width **55.5** x height **82.5** x depth **48.5cm** Seating height **77cm**
⊿	Seat to backrest **134°** Seat to horizontal **0.5°**
🏋	3.85kg
⚒	Magis, Italy

Stool One is a development of Grcic's Chair One (p. 56), the polyhedral design of the chair (Grcic has talked about his 'stealth-bomber aesthetic') adapted to the generic form of a bar stool. Here, however, Grcic has taken his reductive approach one step further. By limiting the number of legs to three and using the inherent strength of the casting to cantilever the seat, he has achieved a high level of visual lightness without compromising stability.

Because the rear stretcher has also been dispensed with, the stool can be stacked in a close formation. Three rubber buffers – two under the seat, one under the foot-rail – prevent the stools from jamming or damaging one another when stacked.

Interestingly, a year before the aluminium Stool One was released, Grcic designed a similar version in plastic: the Miura bar stool for Plank. It was here that he introduced the three-legged form, while deliberately moving on from the faceted planes of his Chair One to a softer, more rounded aesthetic better suited to the gas-assisted plastic moulding process.

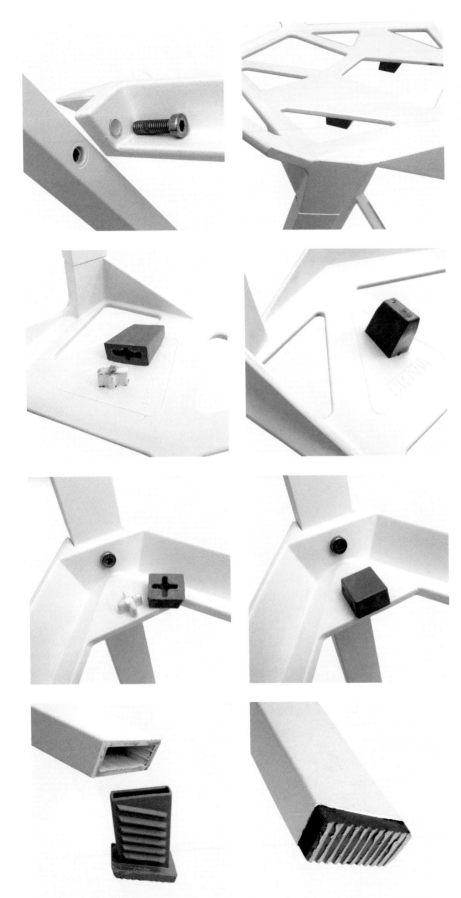

Construction

Seating surface Aluminium die-casting, WT5–6mm.

Legs Rectangular-section aluminium extrusion 18x35mm, WT3.2mm, push-fitted with adhesive to seat-casting. Each leg has one front-mounted M6 steel threaded-rivet insert to attach the footrest.

Footrest V-section aluminium casting, WT6mm, attached with three M6 x 20mm stainless-steel socket-head cap screws using blue locking-paint. Height from floor 340mm at front rising to 370mm at back legs. The strip on the top edge of the footrest is 6mm wide and 3mm higher than the ridge. It is polished free of powder coating to help define the footrest, and to provide a clean line right from the start.

Stacking bumpers Under seat: grey TPE 28.5mm high, 31.5x15.5mm at base, glued and push-fitted on to X-shape casting 20x10x15mm, WT5mm. Under footrest: grey PP, 18.5x21x9mm, glued and push-fitted on to X-shape casting 15x15x7.5mm, WT3mm.

Feet Grey PP moulding, push-fitted, height 34mm, visible foot 4mm.

Surface treatment The aluminium castings are first treated with sputtered fluorinated titanium, then given a semi-gloss powder coating in white or silver. Alternatively, the aluminium is polished then lacquered to show the material's colour.

Superleggera 699

Gio Ponti 1951–57

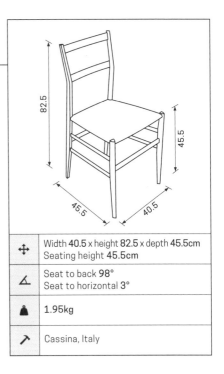

⤢	Width **40.5** x height **82.5** x depth **45.5cm** Seating height **45.5cm**
∠	Seat to back **98°** Seat to horizontal **3°**
⚖	**1.95kg**
⚒	Cassina, Italy

The most distinctive aspect of this chair is not so much its elegant, ladder-backed form but, as its name suggests ('Superleggera' is Italian for 'super light'), its lack of mass. Weighing less than 2kg, it is possibly the lightest wooden chair in production – and was designed more than half a century ago.

Ponti had already been working on updating the traditional chair of the Chiavari region of Italy when he was approached by Cassina to produce a lightweight wooden chair. His first design, the Leggera 646 from 1952, was similar but used round leg sections. Ponti was dissatisfied, and spent years refining the design to reduce the weight still further, eventually using finer dimensions and a triangular leg section to realize his goal.

These reductions required a complex construction for the corner joints of the rails and legs. With so little material available, the rails have to engage not only the legs but also each other, the horizontal and vertical tenons gripping in and around the leg and stabilizing the joint in all three planes (see line drawing on p. 186).

Construction

All parts of frame are made of ash.

Legs Triangular section tapering over length. Front leg: top 27x22mm, middle 32.5x22mm, foot 19x19mm. Rear leg: top 19x18mm, at seat height 33.5x23.5mm, foot 19x18mm. Rear leg angled backwards at lower backrest slat approx. 15°. The rear surface of the front leg is not a flat plane, but varies over its length in a very subtle classical curve, widening at the top to accept the stretchers then narrowing to the foot.

Backrest Two slats 36x7mm.

Stretchers Side stretchers 21x7mm, front and rear stretchers 30mm x 7mm. All stretchers joined with mortice and tenon, tenon approx. 10mm long x 6mm thick.

Seat rails The front and back rails have round pegs, approx. Ø7mm, which engage in the legs, and a flat 7mm tenon to engage in the end of the side rails. The side rails have round-ended tenons approx. 15mm long that engage the leg, and a mortice, chamfered at 45°, to accept the tenon from the side stretchers. The side rails are not parallel, but meet the back legs at an angle, so the tenon on the rear end of the side rail is angled outwards at approx 25°.

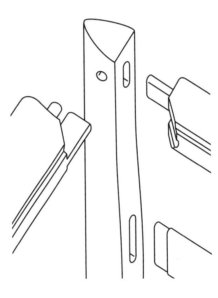

To enable the weaving rattan to be attached, the top inside edges of the rails are rebated approx. 5x5mm. This ledge is used to position a rod of peeled cane, known as the liner (see photo this page, first column, second from top), around which the rattan strips are wound before being led around the rails and across the seat, woven in a twill-weave pattern.

Thinking Man's Chair

Jasper Morrison 1986

⊹	Width **64** x height **72** x depth **96**cm Seating height **35–31**cm
∠	Seat to backrest **103.5°** Seat to horizontal **4.5°**
⬛	12.45kg
⚒	Cappellini, Italy

This seat, complete with a miniature table at the end of each armrest, was originally going to be called the Drinking Man's Chair. However, the slogan on a packet of pipe cleaners that Morrison had bought for model-making – 'The thinking man smokes a Peterson' – prompted him to change the name to something a little more sophisticated. The handwritten dimensions were added as a minimalist form of 'surrogate decoration' for an exhibition in Japan.

Recalling the efforts of a journeyman metalworker, this chair demonstrates most of the standard metalworking techniques: the back legs use free-form bending, the front legs die-form bending, the top corners of the backrest are mitre joints, the spacers between the backrest and arms butt joints. Where the joints are visible, they are very cleanly brazed; where they are not, for example under the circular 'tables', they are more roughly welded.

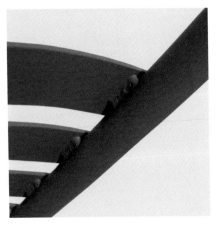
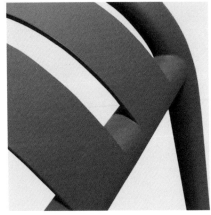

Construction

Legs Ø25mm steel tube, WT2mm, the short spacers between backrest and arms Ø20mm tubes. Rear legs curve forwards to form the armrests and are finished with small 'tables': Ø100mm x 3mm laser-cut steel. Height of tables from ground 595mm. Horizontal gap between inside edges of the two tables (the narrowest dimension of the seating space): 420mm.

Arm supports Ø12mm steel rod.

Seating surface Seven slats of 40x3mm rolled steel.

Backrest Two slats of 3mm steel, tapering minimally from 51.5mm at the side-fixing to 60mm in the centre.

Feet Back: steel oval, WT3mm. Front: turned brass insert, half-domed with Ø15mm flat.

Toledo

Jorge Pensi 1988

The Toledo was designed principally for outdoor use, such as in the cafés of Barcelona, the city in which Jorge Pensi's studio is located. What makes this all-aluminium chair particularly special is the skillful way in which the four organically shaped cast parts have been combined with the geometric extruded legs.

Within the limitations imposed by two-part sand moulds (no undercuts and limited precision), Pensi has achieved a fluid, graceful form. Indeed, the benefits of this casting process – soft radii, sweeping curves and a solidity not found in sheet metal – have been maximized with great sensitivity.

The development of the chair was very much a hands-on process, the designer moving from sketches to models and back again, refining the shape in many 1:1 mock-ups, and working closely with the casting factory. Pensi later revised the design, adapting it for production as a one-piece chair in polypropylene: the Toledo Air. In translating the design to the new process, ensuring that the flow of plastic would be uninterrupted, Pensi once again worked mainly with 1:1 models.

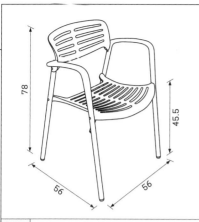

⊹	Width **56** x height **78** x depth **56cm** Seating height **45.5–41.5cm**
⊿	Seat to backrest **102°** Seat to horizontal **6°**
⬛	6.85kg
⌇	Resol, Spain; Knoll, USA (originally Amat-3, Spain)

Construction

Seat, backrest and armrests Sand-cast aluminium, thermo-treated and polished; underside of seat has unpolished casting finish. (See this page, top right, for a photo of seat casting before the casting sprues have been removed.) Backrest approx. WT8mm, rising to 9mm at top edge. Slots taper from approx. 12mm in centre to 9.5mm at outside. Seat: approx. WT8mm, reducing to 6mm at the turned-down edges. Slots taper from approx. 12mm at centre to 10mm at outside edge. Armrest ovoid section 36x18mm, corner radius R50mm.

Fixings Seat and backrest have embedded (cast-in) M6 stainless-steel nuts. In addition, to prevent rotation, the armrest has a small oval tenon approx. Ø10mm flattened to 9mm x 7.5mm high, which engages in a hole approx. Ø10mm (flattened to 9mm) x 9mm deep in the backrest (see photo this page, first column, second from top). Screws: all stainless-steel cylinder-head socket screws, head Ø10mm x 6mm; armrest/backrest M6 x 41mm, seat/legs M6 x 37mm.

Legs Anodized aluminium tube Ø25mm, WT2mm, front 460mm long, back 610mm long. All legs fixed to armrest with M6 x 20mm dome-headed socket screw Ø10.5mm. Armrest extends as solid rod 50mm into back leg, and 75mm into front leg. Back legs contain nylon spacer Ø21mm x 30mm, drilled sideways Ø6mm, ends slotted for orientation during assembly (see photo this page, first column, third from top). This spacer allows the cylinder head of the M6 seat-fixing screw to be flush with the outside surface of the leg.

Feet Grey PE, base Ø25mm x 6mm, slightly domed, insert Ø18mm, WT1.5mm, with three Ø21mm x 2mm ribs.

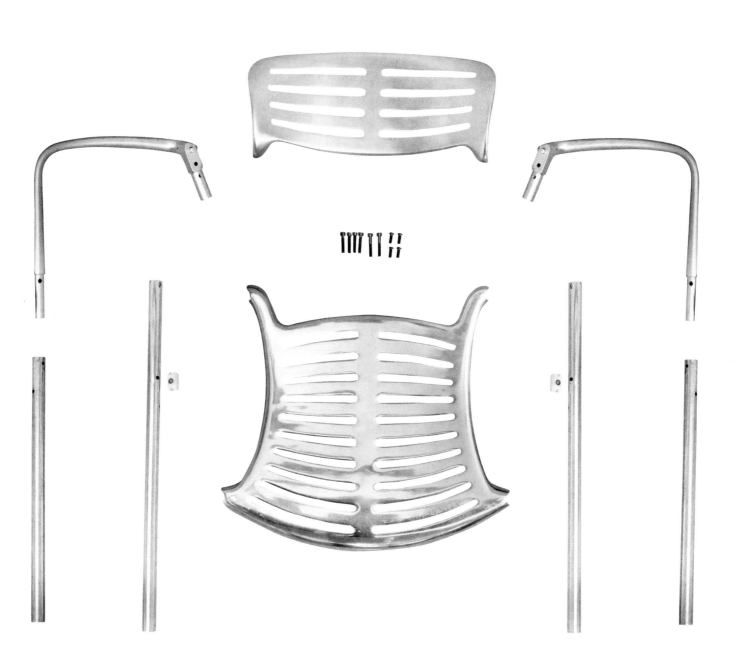

Ulm Stool

Max Bill, Hans Gugelot, Paul Hildiger   1954

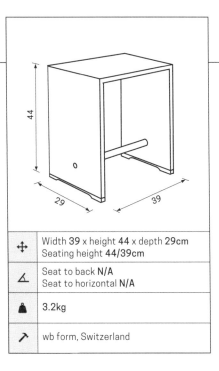

⤢	Width **39** x height **44** x depth **29cm** Seating height **44/39cm**
⊿	Seat to back **N/A** Seat to horizontal **N/A**
⚖	3.2kg
⚒	wb form, Switzerland

As an example of a bespoke design, this stool – possibly the simplest seat in the book – has a very interesting story to tell. It was created for a specific building, and, from the start, was intended as a multifunctional object.

In 1953 the newly founded Hochschule für Gestaltung Ulm (HfG; Ulm School of Design), seen by many as the successor to the Bauhaus, was in need of a seating solution for its seminar rooms, canteen and halls of residence. The school's founding rector, Max Bill, collaborated with one of the teachers, Hans Gugelot, and the woodwork technician, Paul Hildiger, to design an economic solution that could be made in the school's own workshops.

The stool's simplicity belies the many uses to which it can be put: seating at two different heights, in multiples as shelves, as a table, on a table as a lectern, as a carrying tray or a ladder. The fact that Bill, an architect, artist and designer, Gugelot, an industrial designer, and the craftsman Hildiger were working together as a multidisciplinary team helped to reinforce and confirm the educational mission of the school. Gugelot's input can be seen in the stool's formal links to the hi-fi equipment he designed for Braun in 1955: the G-11 radio, the G-12 turntable and the PK-G radiogram.

The first stools were made using Bill's own woodworking machine. Bill then donated the machine to the HfG, enabling it to start production and equip the school with seating.

Construction

Seat and legs Spruce wood, WT 17mm, joined with finger-joints, 8mm wide, 8mm pitch. The bottom edge of the legs (or side walls) has a 0.5mm chamfer to soften the transition to the hardwood skid.

Footrest Beech rod Ø25mm reduced to Ø20mm where it enters the legs. Glued and fixed from the outside with a 3.2mm beech wedge.

Skids Beech 16mm high x 17mm wide, fixed to the legs with a 4.8mm tenon 7mm high. Skid rebated 7mm in the middle section of the bottom side, resulting in four feet, each approx. 50mm long, outside edges shamfered approx 1.5mm.

By giving the footrest a shoulder where it is fixed to the legs, the stool can bear a load when placed on its side, thus offering two heights of seating. The beech skids on the base of the legs, being a harder wood, reduce wear and tear; they also prevent the grain of the legs from splitting out when the stool is dragged over a rough surface.

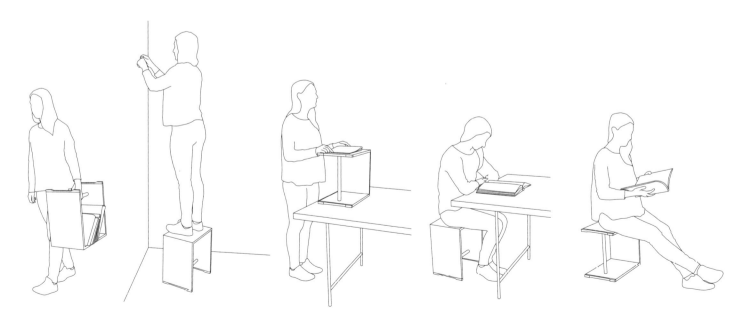

Universale

Joe Colombo 1967

Joe Colombo's Universale was one of the first full-size chairs to be made entirely out of injection-moulded plastic. Colombo's original intention was to offer interchangeable legs for different seating heights. However, the chair proved too unstable when fitted with long legs, such as those for the bar-stool version, so only the standard size was produced. Crucially, the legs remained removable.

One of the benefits of the removable legs was that a smaller moulding tool could be used for the main seating shell, thus reducing production costs. By designing the legs as identical units, a further reduction could be achieved. Despite being hidden within the seat when the legs are attached, the opening at the end of each leg (for the core of the mould) is closed with a half-round lid (see photo on p. 202, centre). These lids provide additional stiffness and stability at the junction of leg and seat.

The overall design of the chair reflects the aesthetics of its time – the friendly, rounded forms of the 1960s – while also incorporating a number of practical features. The unusual recesses or cut-outs at the side of the seating area enable a maximum of three chairs to be stacked, and the hole at the base of the backrest provides a handle for carrying. The latter also allows rainwater to run off when the chair is used outside.

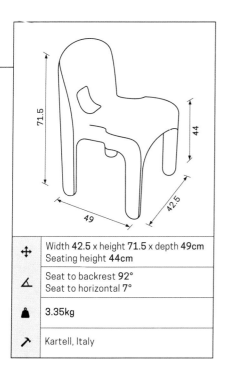

✛	Width **42.5** x height **71.5** x depth **49cm** Seating height **44cm**
⊿	Seat to backrest **92°** Seat to horizontal **7°**
⬛	3.35kg
➤	Kartell, Italy

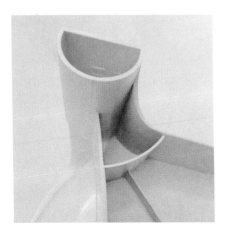

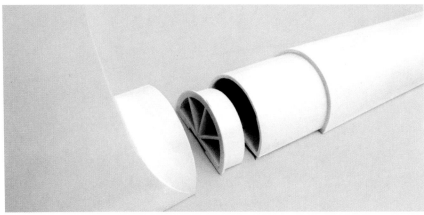

Construction

Seat and backrest One-piece nylon injection moulding, backrest WT 3.5mm, seat WT 4mm, front and side skirts WT 4.5mm, internal stiffening walls WT 3mm. Four leg sleeves on shell WT 3.8mm.

Legs 304.5mm long overall, half-round section 75x44mm, WT 7mm, foot end R40mm, narrower top section 64mm long, WT drops from 4mm to 3.5mm at edge.

Leg closure (lid) WT 2.5mm, stiffening ribs WT 2mm, half-round, depth 20mm.

Feet Transparent PP insert, dome Ø24mm with cut-away segment to match leg profile, push-fitted in Ø14mm hole, 14mm deep.

Initially, the chair was produced in stiff, resilient but costly ABS with the model number 4860. In 1973 a nylon version was introduced, number 4869 (the chair featured here), and the ABS version became number 4868. In 1977 the chair was re-issued in cheaper but more flexible PP with the number 4867.

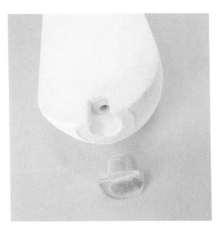

Veryround

Louise Campbell 2006

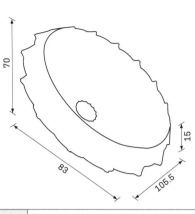

✛	Diam. **105.5** x height **70** x depth **83cm** Seating height **15cm**
◿	Seat to backrest **105°** Seat to horizontal **0°**
♟	11.25kg
⚒	Zanotta, Italy

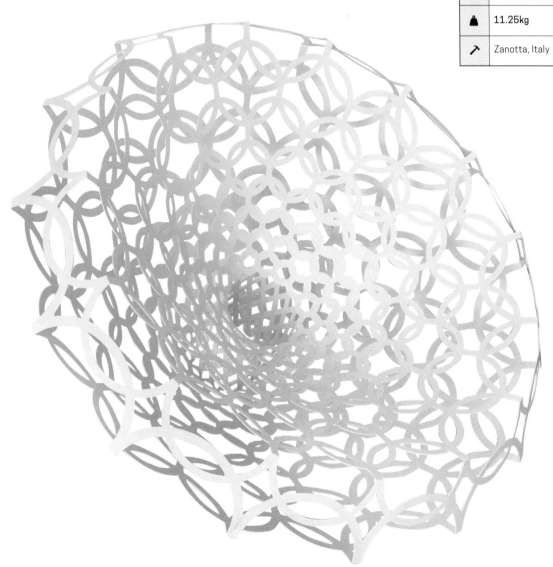

Chairs made entirely out of metal are relatively common, but a chair that has no legs, no defined back or seat, and which rocks not backwards and forwards but from side to side, is unique. Louise Campbell's skill lies not only in designing a chair with these unusual attributes, but also in persuading such an established Italian manufacturer as Zanotta to incorporate it into its collection.

Campbell developed the chair by hand-cutting numerous scale models out of paper, simplifying the design with each new model, and focusing as much on the shadows cast by the form as on the form itself. The final model consisted of 270 circles, which together made up a round, conical shape that convinced the client of the chair's potential. Campbell's associate, Thomas Bentzen, then spent several weeks converting the design into a digital 3D drawing, which was given to Zanotta to develop and put into production. Despite its fragile appearance, the result is stable, relatively comfortable (although Campbell admits it was daring to put aesthetics before comfort) and with an unexpected but playful side-to-side motion.

The chair marks a period in Campbell's work in which she was exploring both decorative forms and new manufacturing processes. In 2001 her Prince chair made use of laser- and water-cutting to achieve a lace-like aesthetic. Two years later, she designed what can be seen as a precursor to Veryround: an extremely graphic, flower-like chair called Billy Goes Zen, with the same form and overall dimensions as Veryround but hand-made in wood.

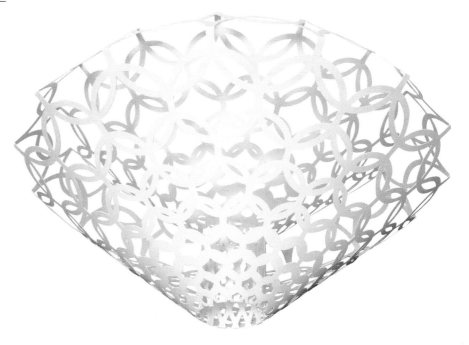

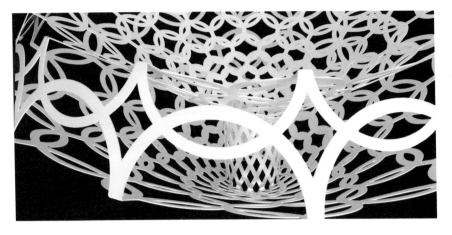

Construction

By using a three-dimensional six-axis laser, as opposed to the more prevalent two-dimensional laser, the manufacturer is able to reverse the usual fabrication process. Here, the circular cut-outs are made *after* the sheet steel has been rolled and welded into cones for the inside and outside chair surfaces. This greatly simplifies the mechanical forming and joining stages, as well as the subsequent cleaning of the weld, as the work is done with a stable sheet of metal, rather than a network of narrow strips. By sequencing the cutting process so that it comes after the forming, the pattern of circles can be placed perfectly within the cones, without any chance of misalignment at the joins.

Outer and inner surfaces 3D-laser-cut sheet steel, WT 2mm. Gap between outer and inner surfaces (height of outside edge) 150mm. Circles vary in diameter in nine steps from 230mm at outer edge down to 51mm at the centre, a reduction of approx. 83% per step.

Central tube 3D-laser-cut sheet steel, WT 3mm, diameter Ø145mm, height 195mm.

All surfaces powder-coated for interior and exterior use.

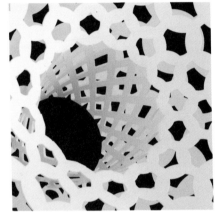

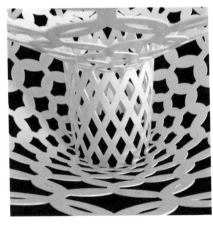

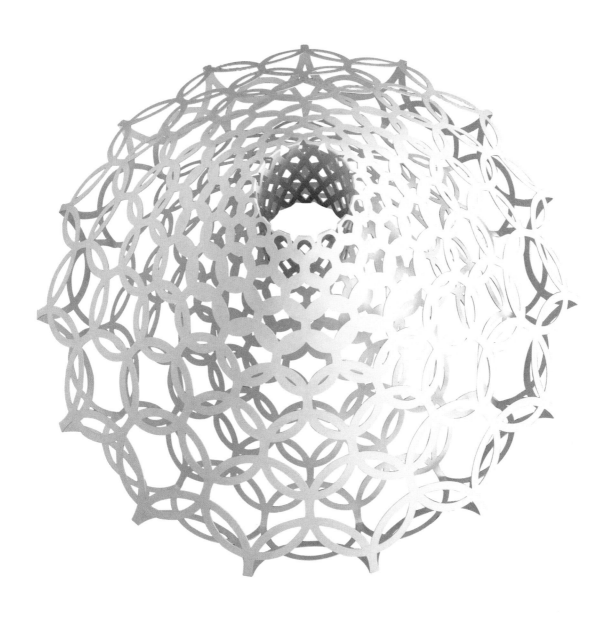

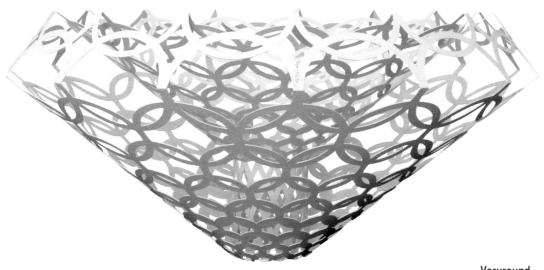

Vilbert

Verner Panton 1993–94

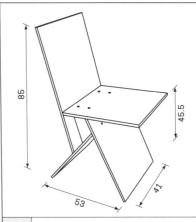

✛	Width **41** x height **85** x depth **53cm** Seating height **45.5–43cm**
∡	Seat to backrest **101°** Seat to horizontal **4°**
🏋	9.5kg
⚒	Ikea, Sweden

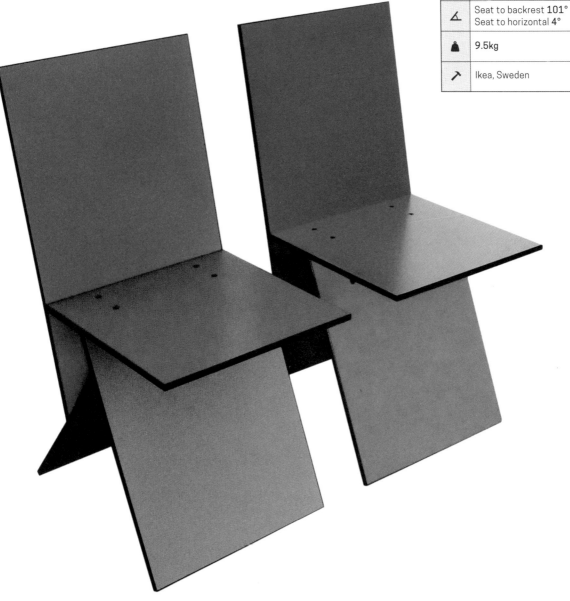

After repeated requests from the French flooring and furniture company Alsapan, Verner Panton designed this chair to promote the company's MDF (medium density fibreboard) panels. He later approached Ikea (he was a good friend of both Ingvar Kamprad, its founder, and Gillis Lundgren, one of its key designers) to see if it was interested in putting it into production. Ikea said it was, and gave it the name Vilbert.

The chair's design represented a return by Panton to the strict geometry of his 1950s furniture, doing away with all superfluous elements, and using a minimum of standard MDF fixings. The result can be seen as a stripped-down embodiment of the flat-pack, build-it-yourself philosophy. In a sense, it was also a realization of another of Panton's preoccupations: the designing of chairs made out of just one material – in this case 10mm MDF, the same panels being used for seat, back and legs, and differing only in their position, angle and length. Two years after the chair's introduction, Panton showed a glass version at the 'Interior Landscape' exhibition at Tommy Lund Galerie in Odense, Denmark.

It is worth noting that two different screws were used: flat-headed in the seat, and countersunk in the backrest – possibly because the flat-headed screws were easier to mount exactly flush with the seating surface, resulting in a cleaner finish.

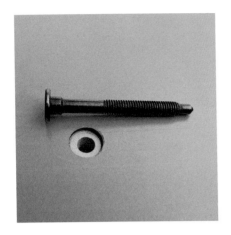

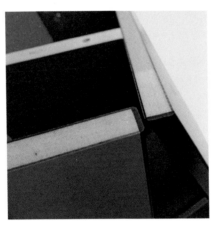

Construction

Seat, back and legs 10mm MDF, covered top and bottom with 1mm melamine laminate (total WT12mm). Outside edges sealed with 2.2mm black ABS. Edging not mitred at corners but overlapping, with shorter lengths overlapping the longer. Central trapezoidal pieces 19mm MDF covered in grey laminate approx. 0.15mm, total WT19.4mm, no edging. Screw holes Ø6.5mm, dowel holes Ø10.5mm.

Seat (red) and back leg (purple) each fixed with four M6 x 60mm cylinder-head socket screws, head Ø13mm x 2mm, neck Ø7mm x 4mm, sitting flush in Ø13.5mm appropriately rebated holes (see photo this page, top left). Backrest (blue) and front leg (green) each fixed with M6 x 35mm CSK socket screws, head Ø11.5mm, sitting 1mm recessed in Ø13.5mm CSK holes. All screws engage in Ø10mm x 14mm steel cross dowels (barrel nuts), threaded M6, located in the central trapezoids (see photo this page, top right). One end of the cross dowel is slotted for orientation when assembling. M6 threaded hole is placed asymmetrically 5.5mm from non-slotted end, as dowels sit in blind holes facing the inside of the chair. This brings the threaded hole in line with the centre of the panel.

Additional angles Seat underside to front leg 67°, front to back leg 65°, back leg to back 127°.

Colours Two versions of the chair were offered, both using the same colours but in different combinations.

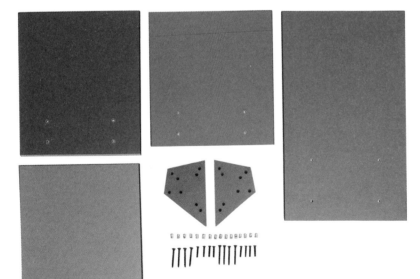

Washington Skin

David Adjaye 2010–13

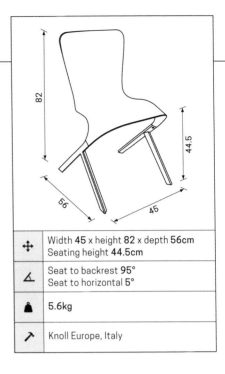

⊹	Width **45** x height **82** x depth **56cm** Seating height **44.5cm**
◺	Seat to backrest **95°** Seat to horizontal **5°**
⬛	5.6kg
↗	Knoll Europe, Italy

David Adjaye's unusual combination of an asymmetric leg form with a cantilevered seat demonstrates a unique constructional approach, reducing the plastic shell to minimum material thickness, concealing the metal reinforcements, but emphasizing and presenting the necessary stiffening ribs. Adjaye has talked about an 'exoskeleton', which almost disappears when the user sits down. The positioning of the ribs was determined by stress analyses of the particular materials used.

The shell is die-cast using two-part moulds, a process that reduces tooling costs but also dictates the parallel orientation of the stiffening ribs. This means that some of the ribs rise from the surface at an angle with an apparent undercut – an effect that is usually avoided on small-scale products, but which here becomes a feature. Interestingly, such candour about production methods does not extend to the use of metal reinforcements in the legs and front corner of the seat. These are essential to the elegant, minimalist form of this moulded-plastic chair, but are hidden from view.

The Washington collection also includes the Skeleton (see p. 214, bottom), an all-aluminium version of the Skin with gaps between the stiffening ribs, which are fewer in number but more heavily dimensioned. In 2014 Adjaye explored a similar cantilever construction in his limited-edition Stool 7, developed for the Standseven charity.

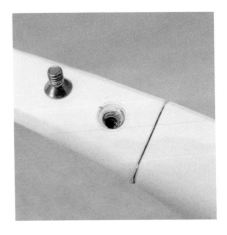

Construction

Seating surface Glass-filled injection-moulded nylon, WT5mm, stiffened with WT3mm ribs on rear surface. In the front corners, two over-moulded cast-aluminium braces with protruding triangular-section tenon, approx. 55mm long, with a two-stage taper, each drilled and threaded M5 once (see photo this page, centre left).

Legs Front and rear leg form a unit. Aluminium casting over-moulded with glass-filled nylon, rear leg 460mm, front leg 320mm joining at 90°, 31mm wide in side view, triangular section 31x28mm at joint, tapering to 31x22mm at foot (7mm 90° champfer on all corners). Top end hollow, approx. 5mm wall thickness, to take aluminium tenon from seat, push-fitted, secured with adhesive and one stainless-steel M6 CSK star-socket screw, Ø10.5mm head, per leg. Right and left leg-units are parallel to each other, i.e. the outside faces are at 90° to the ground.

Feet Leg moulding has a 2.5mm raised skid area recessed 5mm from outside edge at its bottom end.

Surface treatment Seat and legs: matt moulded texture.

Wishbone

Hans J. Wegner 1949

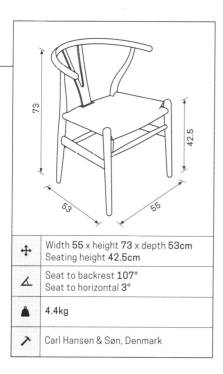

⊹	Width **55** x height **73** x depth **53cm** Seating height **42.5cm**
∡	Seat to backrest **107°** Seat to horizontal **3°**
🏋	**4.4kg**
🛠	Carl Hansen & Søn, Denmark

In 1944 Hans Wegner embarked on a project to explore Chinese chair design. Inspired by the chairs of the Ming dynasty, Wegner produced a series of designs featuring a low backrest with combined armrests. The Wishbone, the last in the series, uses turned and bentwood elements in its construction, in a similar manner to Thonet chairs. Such elements helped to reduce production costs – especially when compared to Wegner's Round chair (see p. 152) with its carved backrest.

The Wishbone, also known as the CH24, was Wegner's first design for the Danish furniture company Carl Hansen. It has been in production since its introduction in 1950, and has sold more units than any of Wegner's other designs.

Construction

Backrest Steam-bent beech, Ø29mm, flattened on front side at centre to 23mm depth, flattened area tapering out to leave the full Ø29mm above the front legs. Central Y-support 65x9mm at seat, splitting into two 26x9mm branches after 100mm height, joined to stretcher with shouldered tenons.

Legs Solid beech, rear Ø39mm at seat height, tapering to Ø21mm at junction with armrest, Ø25mm at foot. Front leg Ø40mm at seat, dome radius at top end, tapering to Ø27mm at foot. Legs joined to seat stretchers with mortise and tenon.

Stretchers Side stretchers 20x39.5mm section at front, tapering to 20x48mm at rear. Front and rear stretchers turned Ø26mm at centre, tapering to Ø17mm at legs.

Seat frame Sides 33x22mm section, front and rear 43x22mm, slotted 5x130mm in front of the Y-support to allow the fixing of the paper cord.

Seating surface Approx. 120m of woven waxed paper cord.

Wood options Beech, oak, ash, cherry or walnut.

Surface treatment Soaped (oak, ash), oil or laquer (all).

Wood

Marc Newson 1988

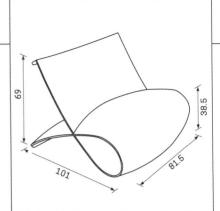

✥	Width **81.5** x height **69** x depth **101cm** Seating height **38.5–29cm**
⊿	Seat to backrest **100°** Seat to horizontal **20°**
🏋	6.9kg
⚒	Cappellini, Italy

Although Marc Newson is known for his work in a wide variety of fields, it is perhaps furniture design in which he is most experimental, especially when it comes to his pieces that test a material to its limits. This chair is unusual for its visual lightness, the simplicity of its construction – just twenty-four strips of wood, with a few horizontal connecting members – and the apparent fragility of its wooden parts.

Wood was originally designed in 1988 as a commission for a Crafts Council of New South Wales travelling exhibition, 'The House of Fiction'. The first version was made by Newson's own company, Pod, using Canadian rock maple and Australian coachwood. Production was then taken over by the English furniture maker James Bradley, who had set up a workshop in Tasmania. Bradley, who had also taught for a while at Newson's old university in Sydney, was keen on using local wood, and produced the chairs in Tasmanian pine.

When Cappellini put the chair into production in the early 1990s, the wood was changed again, this time to beech. The angle of the seat back was also opened up, creating a more reclined seating position.

Construction

The example illustrated here is an early version made from Tasmanian pine.

Seat and backrest Twenty-four strips 16.5x10mm section, bent into a loop or 'alpha' form. At the point where each strip crosses over itself, a Ø4mm x 20mm stainless-steel rod fixes them to form the loop. Total length of the centre strip 2,410mm, the outside strips 2,050mm. Three stretchers within the loop stiffen and stabilize the construction, all 17x17mm. The three stretchers are held to the strips with Ø2.5mm stainless-steel CSK cross-headed woodscrews, head Ø5mm.

Top end-rail Curved section 39x18mm, 795mm long, outside edge half-round Ø9mm. Radius of front edge of rail R1,000mm.

Bottom end-rail Curved and tapered triangular section 795mm long, right-angle triangle 85x67mm in centre, 27x21mm at outside edge. Radius of outside edge R1,010mm.

The strips are held to the two rails with Ø2.5mm stainless-steel CSK cross-head woodscrews, head Ø5mm.

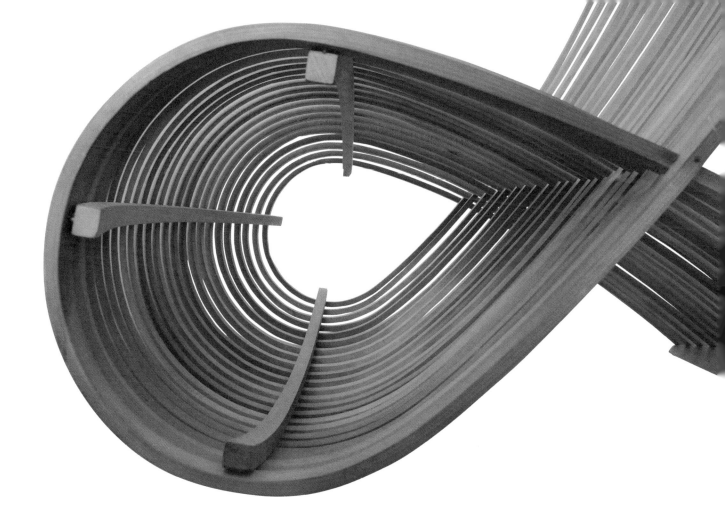

Zig Zag

Gerrit Rietveld 1932–34

In 1927 three examples of the new cantilever chair design were presented to the public: the Rasch brothers' Sitzgeiststuhl, Mart Stam's S 33 (see p. 156) and Mies van der Rohe's MR10 (now sold by Thonet as the S 533). On seeing the chairs, Gerrit Rietveld was struck by their shape, which, rather than enclosing a volume (as a four-legged chair does), seemed to flow through the space of the room. In 1932, drawing on his interest in producing a chair out of a single piece of material, Rietveld began experimenting with the cantilever form using plywood and chipboard, strengthening the design first with a sheet-metal covering, then with a metal edge. Both prototypes are now in the Stedelijk Museum in Amsterdam.

By 1934, Rietveld had come as close to realizing his goal as was technically possible at the time: a single plank of wood, 'folded' at three points, and reinforced with brass screws and small corner wedges. Over the next thirty years, Rietveld's cabinetmaker, Gerard van de Groenekan, produced numerous versions of the chair – in different types of wood (as well as the original oak), with holes in the backrest, with arms, with both holes and arms, and with wedges of different kinds.

In 1971, when Cassina bought the rights to Rietveld's designs, adhesive technology was sufficiently advanced that the screws could be dispensed with, and the wedges minimized and moved right into the corners. Visually, the result is almost exactly the same as Rietveld's second prototype with metal edges.

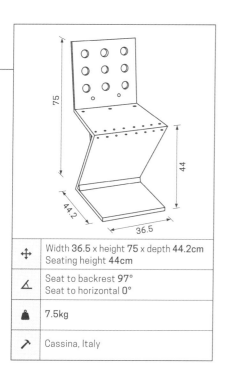

✛	Width **36.5** x height **75** x depth **44.2cm** Seating height **44cm**
∠	Seat to backrest **97°** Seat to horizontal **0°**
⚖	7.5kg
⚒	Cassina, Italy

Construction

The chair illustrated here and on the previous pages is an early model built by Gerard van de Groenekan.

Chair body Four pieces of solid stained elm, all WT20mm. In the historic example shown, each piece is made up of two parts joined with 4mm plywood feathers (visible in one of the backrest holes; see photo this page, first column, second from top). Foot 389mm deep, front edge 291mm wide tapering to 320mm at back edge (approx. 2° taper each side). Seat 364mm wide at front edge, tapering to 319mm at back edge (3.3° taper each side). Backrest parallel, 319mm wide, pierced with nine holes Ø35.5mm. At the top of the rear side is a handgrip rebated 150x20x8mm, approx. radius R10mm, positioned 21mm from top edge, equidistant from sides.

Joints between foot/leg and leg/ seat are mitred and glued with additional triangulated supports (wedges), their outside face 35mm high, WT20mm, inside face positioned 35mm from the corner junction. Joints reinforced with eight (seven at foot/leg) brass BSW ³⁄₁₆ in. (4.7mm) CSK slotted machine screws, with brass square nuts ⁵⁄₁₆ in. (8mm) across flats.

Joint between seat/backrest is a finger-joint. Backrest has three fingers 60mm, 54mm, 60mm wide, seat two fingers 73mm wide, reinforced with five brass BSW ³⁄₁₆ in. dome-headed (dome Ø7.5mm) slotted machine screws, with hexagonal nuts ³⁄₈ in. (9mm) width across flats, sitting within Ø⁵⁄₈ in. (15.5mm) holes – two in the backrest, three in the seat.

Angle foot/leg and leg/seat 47.5°, seat/backrest 97°. The four rubber feet are not original, having been added at a later date.

The Designers

Alvar Aalto p. 128

b. 1898 Kuortane, Finland
d. 1976 Helsinki, Finland

EDUCATION

1916–21 Architecture degree at the Helsinki University of Technology; graduated with distinction

PRACTICE

1921–23 Work experience with Armas Lindgren in Helsinki and Arvid Bjerke in Gothenburg, Sweden

1923 Founded the Aalvar Aalto Office for Architecture and Monumental Art in Jyväskylä, Finland

1928 Joined the Congrès Internationaux d'Architecture Moderne (CIAM)

1933 Moved office to Helsinki

1935 Founded Artek Company and Artek Gallery

1940–48 Research Professor of Architecture at Massachusetts Institute of Technology, USA

Two years after graduating Aalto founded his own office. Shortly afterwards, he married the architect Aino Marsio, who had been in the year above him at same university. Marsio joined his office and they worked together on many projects – especially furniture and interiors – until her death in 1949.

Following the success of the Paimio furniture collection, the Aaltos, together with the art collector Maire Gullichsen and the art historian Nils-Gustav Hahl, founded the company Artek. Their goal, as laid down in the founding manifesto, was 'to sell furniture and to promote a modern culture of habitation by exhibitions and other educational means'. This was emphasized in the company letterhead, part of which read: 'Centre for modern furniture and house fittings, exhibitions of art and industrial art'. In 2013 Artek was bought by the Swiss company Vitra.

Aalto's connection with his alma mater was reinforced when his office won the 1945 competition to plan a new campus for the university at Otaniemi on the outskirts of Helsinki. Later, with his second wife, Elissa, he also designed the main building, completed in 1964, and the campus library. In 2008 the three Helsinki universities, the School of Economics, the University of Technology and the University of Art and Design, were merged and, in his honour, given the name Aalto University.

David Adjaye p. 212

b. 1966 Dar es Salaam, Tanzania

EDUCATION

1984–85 Foundation Diploma in Art and Design, Middlesex University

1990 B.Arch from London South Bank University

1991–93 M.Arch at Royal College of Art, London

PRACTICE

1986–89 Worked at Tchaik Chassay Architects, London

1990–91 David Chipperfield Architects, London, and studio of Eduardo Souto de Moura, Porto, Portugal

1994 Co-founded Adjaye & Russell, London, with William Russell

2000 Established own studio, Adjaye Associates

The son of Ghanaian diplomats, Adjaye spent his early life in Africa and the Middle East before moving to the United Kingdom with his family when he was thirteen.

Adjaye's architecture is renowned for its self-confident use of colour and decorative elements, and for the inclusion of unusual materials. The Washington Collection, Adjaye's first foray into industrially produced furniture, was commissioned by Knoll in 2010 to furnish the National Museum of African American History and Culture in Washington DC. The commision for the building was won in 2009 by the FAB Group, of which Adjaye was the lead designer. The structural reinforcing ribs of the Washington Skin chair refer to the bronze façade of the museum, which is in itself a reference to the casting skills of early African American artisans.

In 2007 Adjaye was awarded an OBE for services to architecture. In 2014 he married the business consultant Ashley Shaw-Scott, who is now head of research at Adjaye Associates.

Edward Barber & Jay Osgerby p. 72

Edward Barber
b. 1969 Shrewsbury, England

EDUCATION

1991 BA Interior Design, Leeds Polytechnic

1994 MA Architecture and Interior Design, Royal College of Art, London

Jay Osgerby
b. 1969 Oxford, England

EDUCATION

1992 BA Furniture and Product Design, Ravensbourne College, London

1994 MA Architecture and Interior Design, Royal College of Art, London

PRACTICE

1996 Founded Barber & Osgerby, London

2001 Founded Universal Design Studio, London

Having studied on the same course at the Royal College of Art, Barber and Osgerby set up their first office in the brutalist Trellick Tower in London. Their initial designs were mostly derived from folding and bending sheet material, a legacy of their architectural model-making in card. In 1997 they showed their plywood Loop Table at the 100% Design Fair in London. The table, which is still in production, was subsequently taken up by Isokon Plus; it also drew the attention of Cappellini. Thus began a close relationship between Barber & Osgerby and the two manufacturers, resulting in many commissions in the following years.

In 2004 the designers won the Jerwood Applied Arts Furniture Prize. Their involvement in the accompanying travelling exhibition organized by the British Crafts Council resulted in a recommendation for the De La Warr Pavilion chair contract – the first of a series of projects for the recently formed Established & Sons.

Mario Bellini p. 48

b. 1935 Milan, Italy

EDUCATION

1959 Graduated in architecture from Polytechnic University of Milan, Italy

PRACTICE

1961–63 Head of design at the La Rinascente chain of department stores

1963 Founded an architectural office with Marco Romano

1962–65 Professor at the College of Industrial Design, Venice, Italy

1982–83 Professor of Architectural Composition at the University of Applied Arts in Vienna, Austria

1987 Founded Mario Bellini Associati, later Mario Bellini Architects, in Milan

In 1961, recently married and unable to find sufficient work as an architect, Bellini took on the role of head of design at La Rinascente department stores, where he was responsible for furniture, furnishings and packaging. Within two years he had won the first of eight Compasso d'Oro design awards, for a plywood table (now reissued under the name Cartesius). Not only was it Bellini's first award, it was also the first Compasso d'Oro to be given for a piece of furniture. This initial success paved the way for Bellini's subsequent career.

Bellini's work covers an enormously wide field, from furniture, lighting and office equipment (he was a consultant to Olivetti between 1963 and 1991) to exhibition design and architecture. He has found success in all these areas, receiving awards, showing his work in international exhibitions and having his pieces accepted into the collections of design museums around the world (the Museum of Modern Art in New York alone has twenty-five of his designs in its permanent collection). In 2017 the Triennale in Milan staged a retrospective of his work entitled 'Mario Bellini: Italian Beauty'.

Max Bill p. 196

b. 1908 Winterthur, Switzerland
d. 1994 Berlin, Germany

EDUCATION
1924–27 Trained as a silversmith at
the Kunstgewerbeschule (School of
Arts and Crafts), Zurich, Switzerland
1927–28 Studied at the Bauhaus
School of Design, Architecture and
Applied Arts, Dessau, Germany

PRACTICE
1929 Freelance architect, painter
and graphic designer in Zurich
1932–33 Designed and built his own
house and atelier
1933 Created first sculptural works
1937 Published first work on
typography: 'Die typografie ist der
grafische ausdruck unserer zeit'
1938 Joined the Congrès Internationaux
d'Architecture Moderne (CIAM)
1944/45 Taught form and
proportion (*Formlehre*) at the
Kunstgewerbeschule, Zurich
1951 Co-founder and architect of the
Hochschule für Gestaltung Ulm (HfG;
Ulm School of Design), Germany
1952–56 Rector and head of the
Department of Architecture and
Product Design, HfG
1967–74 Professor of Environmental
Design, State Academy of Fine Arts,
Hamburg

Despite Bill's relatively short period of
formal education at the Bauhaus (at a
time when Walter Gropius was rector
and Marcel Breuer head of the carpentry
workshop), his career demonstrates
such a wide range of skills that he could
be described as a modern Renaissance
figure. In addition to his architecture
and teaching, Bill worked successfully
as an administrator, sculptor, painter,
graphic designer, industrial designer and
typographer. He was only twenty-three
when, a year after his marriage to the
musician and photographer Binia Spoerri,
he started designing and building his
own house and atelier in Zurich – an
indication not only of his professional
abilities but also of the confidence with
which he approached life.

Ronan & Erwan Bouroullec pp. 68, 176

Ronan Bouroullec
b. 1971 Quimper, France

EDUCATION
1991 Diploma in industrial design,
École Nationale Supérieur des Arts
Appliqués et des Métiers d'Arts, Paris
1995 Diploma in furniture design,
École Nationale Supérieur des Arts
Décoratifs, Paris

PRACTICE
1996 Founded own office
1999 Joint partner with Erwan

Erwan Bouroullec
b. 1976 Quimper, France

EDUCATION
1999 Degree in fine art, École
Nationale Supérieur des Arts
Décoratifs, Cergy-Pontoise, France

PRACTICE
1998 Began assisting Ronan
1999 Joint partner with Ronan

It could be said that the Bouroullecs'
career is marked by their drive to
acquire public recognition. Ronan
Bouroullec began entering competitions
and exhibitions while still a student,
succesfully showing various designs
for domestic interiors – vases, furniture,
lighting. In 1997 this proactive approach
brought the Bouroullecs' their first
significant contract, for Cappellini.
Two new contracts in 2000 – a shop
interior for Issey Miyake in Paris, and
the office-furniture collection 'Joyn' for
Vitra – firmly established them on the
international stage.

Marcel Breuer p. 52

b. 1902 Pécs, Hungary
d. 1981 New York, USA

EDUCATION
1920 Scholarship to study painting
and sculpture at the Academy of
Fine Arts, Vienna; dropped out shortly
after starting
1920–24 Joiner's apprenticeship
leading to journeyman's certificate,
Staatliches Bauhaus, Weimar, Germany

PRACTICE
1924–25 Worked for the furniture
designer Pierre Chareau in Paris
1925–28 Head of the carpentry
workshop (*Jungmeister*), Bauhaus,
Dessau
1928 Founded own architectural of
fice in Berlin
1933–35 Emigrated to Hungary,
then Switzerland
1935 Emigrated to England; founded
architectural office with F. R. S. Yorke
in London
1937–46 Emigrated to the United
States; Professor of Architecture,
Harvard University
1937–41 Architectural office
with Walter Gropius in Cambridge,
Massachusetts
1941 Founded own architectural
office in Boston
1946 Moved office to New York

Breuer's first furniture designs were
in wood, and were strongly influenced
by De Stijl and constructivism; indeed,
the Slatted Chair from 1924 could be
mistaken for a Gerrit Rietveld design.
Breuer's interest in metal furniture arose
during his employment as head of the
Bauhaus carpentry workshop. Inspired
by the construction of his new Adler
bicycle, he attempted to interest the
Adler company in furniture production.
When this failed, he commissioned
Mannesmann, the inventors of seamless
steel tubing, to bend up the parts for
his first designs. The early influence of
Rietveld is still visible in the geometric
reduction of his B3 (Wassily) chair from
1925, a stripped-down, machine-age
version of the classic leather club chair.

In 1926, aged twenty-four, Breuer
married the Bauhaus graduate Marta
Erps, an artist and textile designer.
In that year he also co-founded the
Standard Möbel company in Berlin,
to produce his tubular-steel furniture
designs. Because the Bauhaus was
trying to generate income by producing
and selling designs developed in its
workshops, Breuer's move resulted in
conflict between him and the school's
director, Walter Gropius. However,
Breuer's chairs and stools were
purchased to furnish the canteen and
theatre at the new Bauhaus buildings
in Dessau. In 1929 Standard Möbel
was acquired by Thonet, which is still
producing Breuer's designs today.

Louise Campbell p. 204

b. 1970 Copenhagen, Denmark

EDUCATION
1992 Graduated from the London
College of Furniture
1995 Degree in industrial design
from Danmarks Designskole (now
the Royal Danish Academy of Fine Arts
– The School of Design)

PRACTICE
1996 Founded own office in
Copenhagen
2008–10 Chair of the Committee for
Design and Crafts at the Danish Arts
Foundation
2015 Awarded an honourable lifetime
grant from the Danish Arts Foundation

With an English mother and Danish
father, Campbell was brought up and
educated in both England and Denmark,
which helps to explain her unique
approach to design. Her repertoire
extends from the reduced simplicity of
her wooden November desk for Nikari,
or her cutlery for Georg Jensen, to more
playful, experimental work, such as her
Seesaw or the Random Chair.

In 1997, together with Malene
Reitzel, Campbell co-founded
Kropsholder (Bodyholder), a group of
fourteen female furniture designers.
The group's aim was to develop an
alternative, experimental and poetic
approach to designing furniture within
the framework of the existing industry.
In the same year, Kropsholder presented
its work at the Scandinavian Furniture
Fair in Copenhagen.

In 2015 Campbell was awarded an
honorary grant from the Danish Arts
Foundation for exemplary work as a
designer. Because these grants are
bestowed for life, and only twenty-seven
are available in the area of craft and
design, the presentation of a new grant
is both a rare event and a great honour.

Achille & Pier Giacomo Castiglioni p. 116

Achille Castiglioni
b. 1918 Milan, Italy
d. 2002 Milan, Italy

EDUCATION
1944 Graduated in architecture from Polytechnic University of Milan
1969 Received his doctoral degree (habilitation)
1969–77 Lecturer in architecture at Polytechnic University of Turin, Italy
1977–80 Professor of Interior Architecture at Polytechnic University of Turin
1981 Professor Ordinarius of Interior Architecture at Polytechnic University of Milan

Pier Giacomo Castiglioni
b. 1913 Milan, Italy
d. 1968 Milan, Italy

EDUCATION
1938 Graduated in architecture from Polytechnic University of Milan
1964–68 Professor of Life Drawing at the Faculty of Architecture, Polytechnic University of Milan

PRACTICE
1937–44 Pier Giacomo worked with his brother Livio and Luigi Caccia Dominioni, both architects
1944–68 Achille, Pier Giacomo and Livio co-founded their architecture and design office (Livio left the office in 1952)

In the first few years after establishing their practice, the Castiglioni brothers worked mainly on urban planning, building and industrial-design projects. After Livio's departure, Achille and Pier Giacomo concentrated more on interiors and exhibition design.

Pier Giacomo had first demonstrated an affinity with the avant-garde when, at twenty-six, one year after graduating, he had designed the Fimi Phonola 547 radio with his brother Livio and Luigi Caccia Dominioni. The 547's design was revolutionary in that it did not refer to previous radios, but approached the form from scratch. It questioned all assumptions and preconditions, aiming at a simple, functional, even 'poor' design in terms of the economic use and choice of materials. The brothers applied this same philosophy to their designs of the 1950s and 1960s, creating a new aesthetic by eschewing standard solutions, by simplifying and revealing an object's function, and by using irony to underline or explain the original purpose of the object.

Joe Colombo p. 200

b. 1930 Milan, Italy
b. 1971 Milan, Italy

EDUCATION
1948–55 Studied painting at the Accademia di Belle Arti di Brera, Milan, and architecture at the Polytechnic University of Milan

PRACTICE
1955–63 Worked primarily on architectural projects
1958–61 Took on family business with his brother
1961 Left family business and opened his own studio in Milan
1963–71 Worked primarily on interior architecture, product and furniture design projects

Joe (Cesaro) Colombo's short working life is notable for the creative energy he brought to the many different fields in which he found success: painting, architecture, interior architecture, and product and furniture design. The brief period during which he ran the family electrical business allowed him to both experiment with and develop his design talents. In his clear, accurate sketches, he worked up ideas for products as diverse as wine glasses, wristwatches and storage units (Boby).

From his architectural background, Colombo brought a systematic approach to design, which he combined with a love of everything new and modern. Drawing on ideas from the world of automobiles – both the aesthetics and the production techniques – he strived for a dynamic vision of future living, deliberately ignoring the borders between product, interior and architecture.

Hans Coray p. 96

b. 1906 Zurich, Switzerland
d. 1991 Zurich, Switzerland

EDUCATION
1929 Graduated with a doctorate in romance language studies from Zurich University, Switzerland
1931 Teacher in a middle school, Aarau, Switzerland
1932–38 Studied astrology, design, graphology and religious philosophy

PRACTICE
1930 Began experimenting with furniture design
1941 Taught metalworking courses in Zurich
1945 Freelance artist, sculptor, designer and art dealer

Coray's route into furniture design was not straightforward. His father was director of the Pestalozzi School in Zurich, and later became an art collector and patron. Coray developed a wide range of academic interests, including the arts. In 1931 he married the weaver and painter Verena Loewensberg, who became a member of the Zürcher Konkreten and Allianz artists' groups. As a result, the couple became friends with Max Bill and Hans Fischli, an artist and architect.

In his position as assistant to the head architect of the 1939 Landesausstellung (Swiss National Exhibition, or 'Landi'), Fischli invited Coray to submit designs for the outdoor furnishings. Coray was already involved in preparations for the exhibiton, designing parts of the interiors of the pavilions representing aluminium, chemical and electricity production. It has been suggested that the holes in the Landi chair were inspired by the perforated aluminium sheets used as railings in the aluminium pavilion.

Coray separated from Verena in 1948, having had two children with her. In 1970 he married Henriette Dingetschweiler, who now manages his estate.

Nick Crosbie p. 112

b. 1971 Buckinghamshire, England

EDUCATION
1990–93 BA Industrial Design, Central Saint Martins, London
1993–95 MA Industrial Design, Royal College of Art, London

PRACTICE
1995 Co-founded the design and production company Inflate
2001 First Inflate shop opened in London
2004 Moved away from products towards temporary inflatable architectural structures
2005 D&AD award for Office in a Bucket
2008 Started the AirClad range of temporary mobile architecture
2013 Launched Inflate Works, the official operator of Inflate and AirClad products

Crosbie founded Inflate with two brothers: Mark Sodeau, who worked as the production manager, and the designer Michael Sodeau, who left after four years to set up his own studio. Following the success of the company's small inflatable products, Crosbie became interested in producing bigger objects. In 2004 he created Office in a Bucket, an inflatable, pop-up, open-plan office structure that could be used for any situation requiring semi-enclosed spaces within a larger area.

From the beginning, Crosbie's aim has been not only to design new products, but also to engineer and produce them. The possibility of renting the company's structures led to a new market and the further development of temporary sales and exhibition buildings. More recently, Crosbie helped to develop the Snoozy, a small 'hotel room' for use at festivals and sporting events. He calls this area of quickly built, non-permanent buildings 'fast architecture'.

De Pas, D'Urbino, Lomazzi, Scolari p. 40

Jonathan De Pas
b. 1932 Milan, Italy
d. 1991 Florence, Italy

EDUCATION
1959 Graduated from the Faculty of Architecture, Polytechnic University of Milan, Italy

Donato D'Urbino
b. 1935 Milan, Italy

EDUCATION
1960 Graduated from the Faculty of Architecture, Polytechnic University of Milan

Paolo Lomazzi
b. 1936 Milan, Italy

EDUCATION
1956 Graduated from Athenaeum École Internationale d'Architecture et Design Lausanne, Switzerland

PRACTICE
1966 Founded their own studio, DDL
1967 Designed the first inflatable furniture and temporary buildings
1972 Participated in the exhibition 'Italy: the New Domestic Landscape' at the Museum of Modern Art, New York
1979 Received Compasso d'Oro award for the Sciangai coat stand at the Milan Triennale, Italy

In the early years of their collaboration, De Pas, D'Urbino and Lomazzi worked with the architect Carla Scolari (Lomazzi's wife, about whom little is known) on a number of furniture projects, including some pieces for children (1965), the Blow armchair (1967) and the Brick shelving system (1970). The group's playful, pop-culture approach to furniture design at that time was underlined by Joe (1970) – a giant leather baseball glove.

In 1968 their interest in pneumatic structures had led them to enter an inflatable building in a competition to design the Italian pavilion at the World Fair in Osaka, Japan. In the same year, they were sponsored by Zanotta (the manufacturer of Blow) to design and build a 60-metre-long inflatable linking tunnel at the Triennale in Milan. This was followed by various temporary inflatable structures at Italian trade fairs over the next few years.

DDL was enormously productive from its start, designing and realizing hundreds of products in the areas of furniture and lighting. After the death of De Pas in 1991, the group continued the office under the name Studio D'Urbino Lomazzi.

Charles & Ray Eames pp. 76, 80, 100, 136

Charles Eames

b. 1907 St Louis, Missouri, USA
d. 1978 St Louis, Missouri, USA

EDUCATION

1925–27 Studied architecture at
Washington University, St Louis
(course not completed)

1938 Studied architecture and design
at Cranbrook Academy of Art (CAA),
Bloomfield Hills, Michigan, USA

PRACTICE

1930–36 Architecture with
Charles Grey

1936–38 Architecture with
Robert Walsh

1939 Taught industrial design at CAA

1940 Head of industrial design, CAA

1941 Married Berenice 'Ray' Kaiser

1943 Co-founded Eames Office in
Los Angeles

Ray Eames (née Berenice Kaiser)

b. 1912 Sacramento, California, USA
d. 1988 St Louis, Missouri, USA

EDUCATION

1931–33 Studied painting at the
Bennet School, New York

1933–37 Studied painting at the
Arts Students League, New York, under
the abstract artist Hans Hofmann

1940–41 Studied at CAA

PRACTICE

1941 Married Charles Eames

1943 Co-founded Eames Office
in Los Angeles

Charles and Ray Eames are regarded
as one of the most influential design
partnerships of the twentieth century.
Their work embraced architecture,
film, photography and graphics. Their
practical, experimental approach to the
creation of furniture introduced four new
materials – three-dimensionally formed
plywood, fibreglass, steel wire and
cast aluminium – into the repertoire of
furniture designers.

The partnership began in 1940,
when Charles Eames, together with
Eero Saarinen, won two first prizes at
the Organic Design in Home Furnishings
competition held at the Museum of
Modern Art (MoMA) in New York. Ray
Kaiser, as she was then, was part of
the team preparing Charles and Eero's
competition entries, one of which
was a family of three-dimensionally
formed plywood chairs – the first to
make use of such plywood for seating.
The chairs were in fact upholstered,
meaning that the ply was hidden, as the
forming process could not yet achieve
a veneer with a high-quality surface.
Nevertheless, these chairs would form
the basis of the Eameses' Plywood
Group of chairs, a milestone in modern
furniture design.

The Eameses' second success, in
the 1948 International Competition
for Low-cost Furniture Design, also at
MoMA, enabled them to finance the
development of another new material for
furniture design, fibreglass, resulting in
the Fibreglass or Shell Group of chairs.

Following the Eameses' marriage in
1941, Ray became the stepmother of
Lucia Eames (1930–2014), Charles's
daughter from his first marriage. Lucia
took over the ownership of the Eames
Office in 1988, and in 2004 established
the Eames Foundation.

Konstantin Grcic pp. 56, 180

b. 1965 Munich, Germany

EDUCATION

1985–87 Cabinetmaking course at
Parnham College, Dorset, England

1988–90 Furniture MA, Royal College
of Art, London

PRACTICE

1990–91 Employed by Jasper Morrison,
London

1991 Founded own practice,
Konstantin Grcic Industrial Design
(KGID) in Munich, Germany

Grcic was born in Munich to a German
mother and a Serbian father. In 1985 he
enrolled at Parnham College in south-
west England. The college had been
opened in 1977 by John Makepeace,
a founder member of the British Crafts
Council. With an initial intake of around
ten students per year and a very
intensive, workshop-based timetable,
it provided a concentrated vocational
education for future designer-makers.

After leaving Parnham, Grcic
completed a master's degree in furniture
at the Royal College of Art, presenting
a range of puristic wooden chairs in his
final year. In 2004 the angular aluminium
Chair One for Magis brought him
international recognition.

Grcic, whose work ranges from trade-
fair stands and furniture to lighting and
bottle openers, relies heavily on model-
making. Despite certain drawbacks
inherent to the materials, he develops
his ideas principally through paper and
cardboard models, which he admits
influence his design language.

In 2011 Grcic became involved in
the Young Balkan Designers competition,
run by the cultural organization Mikser
in Belgrade. He regularly presides over
the jury, helping to launch the careers
of young designers from the Balkans
and neighbouring states.

Hans Gugelot p. 196

b. 1920 Makassar, Indonesia
d. 1965 Ulm, Germany

EDUCATION

1940–46 Architecture diploma,
begun at the School of Engineering in
Lausanne, completed at ETH Zurich,
Switzerland

PRACTICE

1946–48 Travel and work in various
architectural offices

1948–50 Employed by Max Bill

1950 Founded his own office; began
developing the M125 furniture system

1954–65 Administrator and lecturer
in design, Hochschule für Gestaltung
Ulm (HfG, Ulm School of Design)

1958 Leader of Development Group II
at the HfG

Gugelot's work is inseparable from
the history of both the HfG and Braun,
the German manufacturer of audio
equipment and household goods.
Gugelot joined the HfG in 1954,
coordinating the completion of the
interiors of the new college together
with the students. Drawing on the
principles of the Bauhaus, the HfG
involved its students in practical and
external projects. By 1958 it had
become necessary to separate teaching
and commercial product design, so
various development groups were
founded, operating as independent
design offices within the college.

It was also in 1954 that Gugelot
had his first contact with Erwin Braun,
who gave him the contract to redesign
his company's entire range of audio
equipment in time for the 1955
Radio Fair in Düsseldorf (Deutschen
Rundfunk-, Phono- und Fernseh-
Ausstellung). This would prove to be
the beginning of a lifelong business
relationship with Braun.

Gugelot's systematic, functionalist
approach to design is apparent in
every aspect of his work, from his first
furniture system, the M125, to the
many products he created for Braun
and the experimental sports car he
was working on shortly before his
death aged forty-five.

Benjamin Hubert p. 140

b. 1984 Maidstone, England

EDUCATION

2003–06 BA Industrial Design
and Technology, Loughborough
University, England

PRACTICE

2006–07 Worked for product-design
consultancy DCA, Warwick, England

2007–10 Senior designer at Seymour
Powell, London, and later Tangerine
Design, London

2010 Founded Benjamin Hubert Ltd,
London

2015 Company restructured to form
industrial-design agency Layer

After graduating, Hubert started working
for one of Britain's largest design
consultancies, David Carter Associates,
renowned for its in-house development
and prototyping departments. Here,
Hubert gained practical experience of
a wide range of technical design skills.
At the same time, he was busy building
his public presence, taking part in
numerous trade fairs and competitions,
and establishing connections with
a variety of European companies. In
2006 he won an award for his lighting
at the New Designers fair; a year later,
he was named best new exhibitor at
100% Design.

Hubert often takes an innovative,
technical production process as the
starting point for a new design – for
example, revealing and exaggerating
the part lines in slip-moulded ceramics
to create an unusual surface aesthetic
or, as in the Pelt chair, exploiting the
possibilities of six-axis milling machines
to create complex joints in wood.

Arne Jacobsen p. 16

b. 1902 Copenhagen, Denmark
d. 1971 Copenhagen, Denmark

EDUCATION

1920–24 Bricklayer's apprenticeship; study trips to Italy and the United States; completed schooling in the building class of the Technical School, Copenhagen
1924 Enrolled at Royal Danish Academy of Fine Arts, Copenhagen
1925 Awarded silver medal at Exposition Internationale des Arts Décoratifs, Paris
1927 Graduated from Architectural School, Royal Danish Academy of Fine Arts

PRACTICE

1927–29 Architect in local-authority planning office, Copenhagen
1929 Founded his own office in Hellerup, Copenhagen

As a child, Jacobsen demonstrated a great talent for drawing and painting. His father, however, steered him away from painting towards the 'safer' profession of architecture. As a student, he assisted his teacher Kay Fisker in designing the Danish pavillion for the 1925 Exposition Internationale des Arts Décoratifs in Paris. There he won a silver medal for his art deco-influenced rattan Paris Chair, originally called Middle Class.

During his extremely productive career as an architect, Jacobsen produced many chair designs, perceiving architecture as a profession that embraces all aspects of buildings, from furniture and lighting to cutlery and ashtrays. One of the best examples of this all-encompassing approach was Jacobsen's design for the Royal Hotel SAS in Copenhagen, for which he also created the Egg and Swan chairs.

In 1927 Jacobsen married Marie Holm, with whom he had two sons. With his second wife, the textile designer Jonna Møller, he developed fabrics and wallpaper during their wartime exile in Sweden.

Pierre Jeanneret pp. 60, 88

b. 1896 Geneva, Switzerland
d. 1967 Geneva, Switzerland

EDUCATION

1913–21 Architecture diploma at the École des Beaux Arts, Geneva, Switzerland (interrupted by First World War, 1915–18)

PRACTICE

1921–23 Worked for Auguste and Gustave Perret, Paris
1922 Co-founded architectural office with Le Corbusier, Paris
1927 Charlotte Perriand joined office as partner
1940 Ended partnership with Le Corbusier
1944 Opened new studio with Georges Planchon, Paris; projects with Charlotte Perriand and Jean Prouvé
1950–65 Collaborated with Le Corbusier on planning the new city of Chandigarh, India
1951–65 Director of the Chandigarh School of Architecture, India

Jeanneret was thirty-six years old when he and Le Corbusier – his cousin – founded their architectural office in Paris. Together they were responsible for such projects as houses 13–15 at the Weissenhof Estate in Stuttgart. By the time they were joined by Charlotte Perriand, there were six young architects from all over the world assisting the cousins. It appears that, among the partners, Jeanneret had the role of studio manager; Le Corbusier was responsible more for acquisitions and the studio's public image.

Over the years, Jeanneret and Perriand became close friends, and he continued working with her on projects after she left the partnership in 1937. In 1940, over a disagreement with Le Corbusier about his position towards the German occupation of France, Jeanneret quit the office himself and joined the French resistance. In the early 1950s, however, he collaborated with Corbusier again, planning the new city of Chandigarh in northern India. Jeanneret designed not only the housing but also the furniture, for government offices and both student and private housing. The furniture demonstrates the influence of his earlier projects with Prouvé and Perriand.

Kaare Klint p. 160

b. 1888 Frederiksberg, Denmark
d. 1954 Copenhagen, Denmark

EDUCATION

1902 Apprenticeship as cabinetmaker
1903 Enrolled on painting courses at the Technical University, Frederiksberg, and studied architecture under the architects P. V. Jensen-Klint (his father) and Carl Petersen

PRACTICE

1914 Produced his first furniture design, a chair for the new Faaborg Museum
1920 Freelance architect
1923 Helped found the Furniture School of the Royal Academy of Fine Arts, Copenhagen
1924 Professor in the Furniture School
1921–26 Responsible for the conversion of the Frederiks Hospital into the Designmuseum Danmark, Copenhagen
1944 Professor of Architecture at the Royal Academy of Fine Arts, Copenhagen

Although Klint's earliest work dates from a period that falls between art nouveau and modernism, his furniture designs are marked by their simplicity and rationality. In contrast to the designers of the Modern Movement, he had a great respect for craftsmanship and a strong feeling for historical context. He also admired the beauty and functionality of Shaker designs and English furniture of the eighteenth century.

Klint was one of the first designers explicitly to consider the ergonomic aspects of seating, researching at great length the proportions and dimensions of the human body and existing furniture. His design practice was based on functional analysis, which took into account ergonomics, construction methods, materials and production processes. His aim was to design furniture that fitted both its purpose and the user, with form and function in balance. Klint named this concept *humanistisk design* – humanist design.

Le Corbusier pp. 60, 88

b. 1887 La Chaux-de-Fonds, Switzerland
d. 1965 Roquebrune-Cap-Martin, France

EDUCATION

1902–04 Began training as an engraver and ornamental metalworker at the École d'Art in La Chaux-de-Fonds, Switzerland
1904–07 Moved to the advanced decorative arts course at the same school

PRACTICE

1905 Produced first architectural work while still at school
1907–11 Work and travel in Europe
1908 Part-time draughtsman for Auguste and Gustave Perret, Paris
1910 Worked for architect Peter Behrendt, Berlin
1913 Completed art teacher's certificate; teaches architecture and interior design at his old school in La Chaux-de-Fonds
1917 Opened first architectural office in Paris
1922 Co-founded architectural office with his cousin Pierre Jeanneret, Paris
1927 Charlotte Perriand joined office as partner
1940 Pierre Jeanneret left partnership
1950–65 Collaborated with Pierre Jeanneret on planning the new city of Chandigarh, India

Charles-Édouard Jeanneret-Gris, who adopted the name Le Corbusier (the crow) in his early thirties, had no formal architectural qualification. During the latter part of his schooling, the director of the advanced decorative arts course, the painter Charles l'Eplattenier, introduced him to architecture and furthered his interest. Le Corbusier's first architectural work, undertaken at the age of eighteen in collaboration with the architect René Chapallaz, was drawing the plans for a villa to be built in a vernacular style. His time with Auguste and Gustave Perret, early pioneers of building in concrete, would influence his later architectural projects.

Furniture design played a relatively small part in Le Corbusier's career. After 1937, the year in which Charlotte Perriand left the office he had founded with Pierre Jeanneret, where she had been the partner responsible for furniture, it would be twenty years before Le Corbusier designed a range of furniture of his own: a *tabouret* (low stool), a circular table and a simple oak desk (now known and sold as LC14, LC15 and LC16) for Le Cabanon, the hut he had built on the French Riviera.

Ross Lovegrove p. 84

b. 1958 Penarth, Wales

EDUCATION

1980 BA Industrial Design, Manchester Polytechnic, England
1983 MA Industrial Design, Royal College of Art, London

PRACTICE

1983–85 Frogdesign, Altensteig, Germany
1985–86 Consultant for Knoll International, Paris
1986 Co-founded Lovegrove & Brown, with Julian Brown, London
1990 Founded own practice, Studio X, in London
2003 Awarded title of Royal Designer for Industry by the Royal Society of Arts, London

After completeing his MA, Lovegrove moved to Germany to work for Frogdesign, one of Europe's leading design studios, which had recently secured Apple as a major client. Three years later, after a spell in Paris, he moved back to London, co-founding Lovegrove & Brown with a fellow RCA alumnus, Julian Brown, who had worked for Porsche Design in Austria after graduating. This partnership lasted four years before the two designers set up their own independent offices.

Lovegrove, a representative of the organic-design revival, was an early user of computer-aided design, employing it to produce the complex, three-dimensional forms he favours. His office has won numerous design award for a wide variety of products, including lighting, furniture, bicycles, cars and aeroplane seats. He is very interested i new materials and innovative productio techniques, and often draws inspiratior from the latest technology, as well as the natural world at both the macro- and the microscopic scale.

Enzo Mari pp. 164, 168

b. 1932 Novara, Italy

EDUCATION

1952-56 Studied art and literature at the Accademia di Belle Arti di Brera, Milan, Italy

PRACTICE

1956 Opened own studio in Milan

1957 Started designing for Danese

1963 Taught at the Scuola Umanitaria, Milan

1963 Joined the Nuova Tendenza artists' movement

1976-79 President of the Associazione per il Disegno Industriale (ADI)

1989 Founded Enzo Mari e Associati in Milan

2000 Awarded title of Honorary Royal Designer for Industry by the Royal Society of Arts, London

2003 Worked for Muji, Japan

Mari's route into the world of design was somewhat unusual, having received no formal training, and with skills that were entirely self-taught. From the beginning, he based his approach on the principle of good, affordable and functional design for all.

While still at university, Mari became interested in the role of the designer in society. After graduating, he set up his own studio and began to investigate the psychology of vision, systems of perception and design methodologies, writing and publishing on these subjects. He also started working as a freelance designer, initially for Danese. Mari's first product for the Italian company was 16 Animali, a wooden puzzle for children, which was followed by various household objects in plastic. This work gave him experience of injection-moulding, enabling him to tackle such furniture projects as the Box chair, designed for Castelli in 1975/76.

With the Box, Mari translated his love of puzzles into a new form. The backrest (in injection-moulded polypropylene) and the legs and back-posts (six connecting metal tubes) could be disassembled and packed into the box-like seat (also in injection-moulded polypropylene). The packaging, too, was a social statement: a simple plastic carrier bag with a cardboard instructions inlay.

In 2003, aged seventy-one, Mari was invited by Muji to design furniture for its 'WORLD Muji' project, which also included work by such younger designers as Sam Hecht and Konstantin Grcic.

Jasper Morrison pp. 20, 36, 188

b. 1959 London, England

EDUCATION

1979-82 BA 3D Design, Kingston Polytechnic, London

1983-84 Scholarship at the Universität der Künste, Berlin

1982-85 M.Des. in furniture design, Royal College of Art, London

PRACTICE

1986 Opened Office for Design in London; first furniture designs produced by SCP, London

1987 'Reuters News Centre', an installation sponsored by Reuters at Documenta 8, Kassel, Germany

1988 'Some New Items for the Home', installation at DAAD Galerie, Berlin

1989 'Some New Items for the Home, Part II', installation in collaboration with Vitra at the Salone del Mobile, Milan

2002 Opened second studio, in Paris

2007 Opened third office, in Tokyo

Well known for his minimalist approach and apparently simple designs, Morrison works in a wide range of fields. He received his early education at Bryanston School in south-west England, where woodworking and Latin were of equal importance. While still at Bryanston, Morrison visited an exhibition of the work of the Irish-born architect and furniture designer Eileen Gray. It was at this exhibition that he realized that designing furniture, with its scale and scope lying somewhere between architecture and engineering, was what interested him most.

From the beginning of his undergraduate studies, Morrison drew inspiration from as many different sources as possible. A regular visitor to the Milan furniture fair, where he saw the debut exhibition of the Italian design and architecture group Memphis, he began making contact with other young Italian and German designers. His first exhibition of plywood furniture, 'Some New Items for the Home', held in Berlin in 1988, attracted the attention of Vitra, which subsequently sponsored a follow-up exhibition in Milan a year later. It also started producing one of the items from Morrison's collection, the Ply Chair.

Marc Newson pp. 124, 220

b. 1963 Sydney, Australia

EDUCATION

1984 BA Sculpture and Jewelry Design, Sydney College of the Arts

1984 Awarded grant from Australian Crafts Council

PRACTICE

1987-91 Lived and worked in Tokyo

1991-97 Lived and worked in Paris

1997 Co-founded Marc Newson Ltd in London with Benjamin de Haan

2006 Awarded title of Royal Designer for Industry by the Royal Society of Arts, London

2012 Appointed a CBE

Shortly after graduating, Newson was awarded a grant from the Australian Crafts Council, enabling him to stage his first solo exhibition: 'Seating for Six', held at Sydney's Roslyn Oxley9 Gallery in 1986. The show included Newson's first self-made LC1 chaise longue – a rounded, organic form made of fibreglass-coated polyurethane foam (a combination of materials used in surfboard construction), which he had given a skin of small, hand-beaten, riveted aluminium plates, reminiscent of 1950s aeroplanes.

Acquired by the Art Gallery of South Australia, this was the piece that launched Newson's career. In 2015, one of the reworked versions from 1988 (named Lockheed Lounge) became the most expensive chair ever sold, reaching more than £2 million at auction. Another chair from Newson's first exhibition, the Cone, which also features riveted aluminium, can be seen in Sydney's Powerhouse Museum. Today, Newson's design work spans an enormously wide range of fields, from watches to aircraft interiors, shoes to shopfittings, bicycles to cameras.

Verner Panton pp. 132, 208

b. 1926 Brahesborg-Gamtofte, Island of Fünen, Denmark

d. 1998 Copenhagen, Denmark

EDUCATION

1944-47 Technical University, Odense, Denmark

1947-51 Architecture degree at the Royal Academy of Arts, Copenhagen

PRACTICE

1950-52 Worked for Arne Jacobsen in Copenhagen

1953 Extended research trips around Europe, interspersed with freelance architectural work and exhibition design

1955 First chair design, Tivoli, put into production by Fritz Hansen

1956 Participated in the competition Neue Gemeinschaft für Wohnkultur; entry included S Chair

1958 Extended and redesigned his parent's Kom-igen (Danish for 'come again') guest house on the Island of Fünen; interiors included his Cone chair

1959 Cone chair put into production by Plus-Linje

1965 S Chair put into production by Thonet

1967 Panton Chair put into production by Herman Miller/Vitra

After only two years of permanent employment, Panton set off around Europe in a VW camper van that he had converted into a mobile drawing office. His goal was to get to know the international design scene, and to establish contacts with manufacturers, dealers and other designers. He was very successful in his aims: the trips resulted in numerous design and architectural contracts, laying the foundations for his future career.

Panton was an immensely creative designer, working on hundreds of lighting, furniture, textiles and interiors projects over the years, not stopping even when he entered his seventies. His Cone series is now produced by Vitra. In 1964 he married Marianne Pherson-Oertenheim, who became his lifelong partner, business manager and promoter.

Jorge Pensi p. 192

b. 1946 Buenos Aires, Argentina

EDUCATION

1965-73 Architecture degree, Facultad de Arquitectura, Universidad de Buenos Aires, Argentina

PRACTICE

1975 Emigrated to Spain; adopted Spanish nationality

1977 Co-founded Grupo Berenguer in Barcelona

1984 Founded Jorge Pensi Design Studio in Barcelona

1990 Office relocated to the Olympic Village in Barcelona

Shortly after arriving in Spain, Pensi founded the design research group Grupo Berenguer in partnership with the Argentinian designer Alberto Liévore and the theoreticians Norberto Chaves (also Argentinian) and Oriol Pibernat (from Barcelona). Specializing in design education and practice, the group took its name from the address of its office: Plaça de Ramon Berenguer el Gran, Barcelona.

In 1984 Pensi set up his own studio, which grew more slowly. After three years he persuaded Diego Slemenson to join him. A young Argentinian architect, jeweller and design theoretician, Slemenson had been introduced to the Grupo Berenguer by Chaves, his teacher, and had already collaborated with the group as a freelancer. Slemenson became heavily involved in the development of Pensi's Toledo chair. He built and shaped the many models and prototypes in card, wood, foam, steel and aluminium, and followed the design through to production, overseeing the casting and adapting the form accordingly.

Pensi is married to the graphic designer Carmen Casares, with whom he collaborates on graphics-related projects.

Charlotte Perriand pp. 60, 88

b. 1903 Paris, France
d. 1999 Paris, France

EDUCATION
1920–25 Diploma in interior design at the École de l'Union Centrale des Arts Décoratifs, Paris

PRACTICE
1925–27 Self-employed; designed furniture and interiors
1927–37 Partner of Le Corbusier and Pierre Jeanneret
1931–34 Study trips to Soviet Union
1937–40 Self-employed; various architectural and furniture projects with Jean Prouvé and Pierre Jeanneret
1940–41 Design consultant to the Imperial Ministry of Trade and Industry, Tokyo, Japan

In her final year at college, Perriand won a competition to take part in an international trade fair in Paris. On graduating, her tutors advised her to launch her career by having stands of her own at the next such fairs. Using money borrowed from her parents, she had her designs made up, exhibiting and selling them at the Salon des Artistes Décorateurs of 1926 and 1927. In the latter year, she also showed at the Salon d'Automne, successfully presenting an ultra-modern metal-and-glass bar (Bar Sous Le Toit), replicating the interior she had installed in her own flat.

After reading Le Corbusier's *Vers une architecture* (1923), Perriand was inspired not only to learn about architecture but also to work for Le Corbusier himself. Perriand's portfolio, together with her stand at the 1927 Salon d'Automne, convinced Le Corbusier to offer her a partnership in the office he had co-founded with Pierre Jeanneret, in a role 'responsible for the atelier's furniture and furnishings programme'.

Perriand's first task was to design a range of modern furniture to replace the standards (from Maple and Thonet) previously specified in Le Corbusier's projects. Of the nine types of chair envisaged by Le Corbusier, each one intended to satisfy a different seating position, Perriand's existing designs covered five (plus a sixth, the Grand Confort, in sketch form). The production of the chairs had been paid for by her then husband, Percy Scholefield.

In 1928, at the end of the initial design process, Perriand presented the Fauteuil à Dossier Basculant, Chaise Longue and Grand Confort in her own flat, adding two of her previous designs (a pivoting chair and bathroom stool) to round off the collection. It was a great success, and all the chairs were taken up by Le Corbusier and Jeanneret in the office's programme. Regrettably, Perriand's major contribution to the creation of these pieces is only now becoming general knowledge, having been overshadowed by her erstwhile mentor, Le Corbusier, for decades.

Gio Ponti p. 184

b. 1891 Milan, Italy
d. 1979 Milan, Italy

EDUCATION
1913 Started architecture degree at the Polytechnic University of Milan
1916–18 Captain in the Italian army
1921 Graduated in architecture from the Polytechnic University of Milan

PRACTICE
1921 Set up studio with the architects Mino Fiocchi and Emilio Lancia, Milan
1923–30 Artistic director at porcelain manufacturer Richard Ginori
1925 Designed his first house, for his family
1926 Co-founded Studio Ponti e Lancia in Milan with Emilio Lancia
1928 Founded *Domus* magazine
1933 Established Studio Ponti-Fornaroli-Soncini with the engineers Antonio Fornaroli and Eugenio Soncini
1936–61 Taught interior design, furniture design and decoration at Polytechnic University of Milan
1940 First collaboration with Cassina
1952 Went into partnership with architect Alberto Rosselli, creating Studio Ponti-Fornaroli-Rosselli

When he started his architecture degree in Milan, Ponti was already in his early twenties. Three years later, in 1916, he was called up for military service, and by the time he had completed his degree after the war, he was thirty years old. His first position was working with Mino Fiocchi and Emilio Lancia, having met the latter during his military training. In 1926 Lancia and Ponti founded a new studio together, with Ponti going on to become one of Italy's best-known architects.

Ponti saw himself as a universal designer, with contracts for furniture, household goods and glassware, as well as in his principal area of architecture. His La Cornuta coffee machine, created for La Pavona in 1948, proved a landmark design, its expressive form helping to redefine post-war Italian culture.

Jean Prouvé pp. 28, 172

b. 1901 Paris, France
d. 1984 Nancy, France

EDUCATION
1916–19 Apprenticed as a blacksmith to Émile Robert, Enghien, Belgium
1919–21 Apprenticeship at the Szabo Smithy, Paris
1921–23 National military service

PRACTICE
1924 Founded own workshop in Nancy, France
1929 Produced his first furniture
1931 Founded own public limited company, Société Les Ateliers Jean Prouvé
1947 Opened larger manufacturing company, Les Ateliers Jean Prouvé, in Maxéville, France
1957 Company bought out by larger firm; worked as freelance architect in Paris
1958–71 Professor of Architecture at the Conservatoire National des Arts et Métiers (CNAM), Paris

Although Prouvé never actually studied architecture, the majority of his immensely productive life was spent in this field. His rational, engineering-based approach often aimed at a systematic form of building, mostly using prefabricated parts in metal. Prouvé's furniture designs reflected not only his love of that material but also his eagerness to experiment with and test new ideas. In developing his designs, he moved constantly between his workshop and studio – repeatedly drawing, making and testing – until the design was considered ready for production.

Ernest Race pp. 24, 32

b. 1913 Newcastle, England
d. 1964 London, England

EDUCATION
1932–35 Interior design degree at the Bartlett School of Architecture, London

PRACTICE
1935 Model-maker
1936–37 Draughtsman at modernist lighting company Troughton & Young
1937–39 Founded Race Fabrics in Knightsbridge, London, selling his own textile designs
1939–45 Served with the Auxiliary Fire Service in London
1945 Co-founded Ernest Race Ltd, with Noel Jordan
1946 Aluminium chairs shown at the exhibition 'Britain Can Make It', Victoria and Albert Museum, London
1948 Received honourable mention for his storage units at the International Competition for Low-cost Furniture Design held at the Musuem of Modern Art, New York
1951 Designed seating for the Festival of Britain, London
1962 Retired as director of Ernest Race Ltd to work on freelance projects; company renamed Race Furniture Ltd

During what was a relatively brief working life, Race managed to produce a large number of very successful, innovative designs. Shortly before the start of the Second World War, the twenty-two-year-old Race travelled with his aunt, a missionary, to Madras in India, where she ran a village weaving business. He spent four months there, designing textiles and carpets to be produced in the village.

After returning to England, Race opened a shop in London to import and sell his India-made designs. His work proved very popular, especially among such modernists as Walter Gropius and Jack Pritchard (director of Isokon), both of whom he had met during his time at Troughton & Young.

In 1945 Race responded to a newspaper advert for a furniture designer. This led to the next stage of his career and the creation of such chairs as the BA3 and the Antelope. As well as his metal-frame seating, Race occasionally produced chairs in plywood, including his redesign of the classic deck chair for the P&O shipping company in 1952–53. The Neptune, as it was called, was an innovative, foldable, two-part construction with laminated legs, held together with webbing straps.

Gerrit Rietveld pp. 148, 224

b. 1888 Utrecht, the Netherlands
d. 1964 Utrecht, the Netherlands

EDUCATION

1899–1906 Apprentice cabinetmaker
in his father's workshop
1906 Draughtsman for the goldsmith
C. J. A. Begeer; also studied
architecture and drawing at the
Municipal Evening School, Museum
of Applied Arts, Utrecht
1911–12 Joined the artists' group
Kunstliefde
1918 Became a member of De Stijl,
the newly founded group of Dutch
abstract artists

PRACTICE

1917 Founded own cabinet-making
workshop in Utrecht
1919 Opened own architectural office
in Utrecht
1924–25 Designed the Schröder House
in Utrecht, following De Stijl principles

Before he began to concentrate on
architecture, Rietveld experimented
with constructivist furniture. This was
the First World War, however, and his
designs were not a commercial success.
In 1917 he took on the then fourteen-
year-old Gerard van de Groenekan as an
apprentice in his workshop. Groenekan
took over the running of the workshop
in 1923, and would spend the rest of
his working life assisting Rietveld and
building his furniture.

In 1927 Rietveld began designing
furniture using steel tubing and metal or
wood in sheet form. This preoccupation
with surfaces resulted in the Zig Zag
chair of the early 1930s and, ten years
later, the Aluminium Chair, an armchair
made from a single sheet of aluminium.

Mart Stam p. 156

b. 1899 Purmerend, the Netherlands
d. 1986 Goldach, Switzerland

EDUCATION

1917–19 Carpentry apprenticeship,
then studied for a diploma in drawing
instruction at the Royal School for
Advanced Studies, Amsterdam

PRACTICE

1919–22 Worked for the architect
Granpré Molière in Rotterdam,
the Netherlands
1922/23 Worked for the architects Max
Taut and Hans Poelzig in Berlin, Germany
1923–25 Worked for the architects
Karl Moser in Zurich and Johannes Itten
in Thun, Switzerland
1926–28 Worked in the architectural
office of Brinkman & Van der Vlugt,
Rotterdam, the Netherlands
1927 Designed three terraced houses
and a cantilever chair for the Weissenhof
Estate in Stuttgart, Germany
1928–30 Taught urban planning
as a guest lecturer at the Bauhaus
in Dessau, Germany
1930–34 Worked in the Soviet Union,
planning new towns at Magnitogorsk
and Orsk
1939–48 Director of the Amsterdam
School of Arts and Crafts, which later
became the Rietveld Academy

Although well known for his tubular-steel
cantilever chair and, to a lesser extent,
his buildings, Mart Stam had little
formal training in either furniture design
or architecture. After completing his
studies to become a drawing instructor,
Stam worked in a variety of European
architectural offices before being
invited by the Deutscher Werkbund
to take part in the 1927 Weissenhof
Estate project, an exhibition of modern
housing in Stuttgart. Stam developed
his cantilevered chair so that his
contribution to the exhibition would be
furnished with suitably modern designs.

Stam was very interested in socialist
architecture and town planning, and
became a founding member of the
Congrès Internationaux d'Architecture
Moderne (CIAM). As one of the 'May
Brigade', a group of socially concerned
architects organized by the German
architect and city planner Ernst May,
Stam spent four years in the Soviet Union
planning new towns at Magnitogorsk
and Orsk. It was there that he met Lotte
Beese, the first woman to have studied
architecture at the Bauhaus. They
married in Moscow before returning to
Amsterdam, where they lived and worked
together for the next ten years.

Philippe Starck p. 108

b. 1949 Paris, France

EDUCATION

1966–69 Studied interior architecture
and product design at the École
Camondo, Paris (course not completed)

PRACTICE

1969 Self-employed; designed
inflatable objects
1971–72 Artistic director at Studio
Pierre Cardin
1976 Designed La Main Bleue nightclub,
Paris; founded Starck Product
1978 Designed Les Bains Douches
nightclub, Paris
1979 Starck Product renamed Ubik
1983 Designed furniture for private
residence of French president, Élysée
Palace, Paris

Starck's father, André, was a well-
respected aeronautical engineer and
inventor. He encouraged his only child
to develop his drawing skills, and to
dismantle and reassemble mechanical
objects for fun – instead of playing
with toys.

Out of a mixture of frustration and
impatience, Starck decided to abandon
his degree course at the private
Camondo design school and begin his
career as a designer. He had already
begun designing and producing inflatable
objects, including a large house for Lino
Ventura's Perce-Neige charity.

These projects attracted the
attention of the fashion designer Pierre
Cardin, who employed Starck as the
artistic director of his studio. However,
it was Starck's designs for two exclusive
Parisian nightclubs that marked the
turning point in his career, bringing him
widespread public recognition. The
commission from the French president
François Mitterrand to decorate the
private residence at the Élysée Palace
secured his international reputation.

Since then, Starck's office has
produced hundreds of designs in a wide
range of fields, including architecture,
interior architecture, furniture, lighting
and household goods.

Harry Thaler p. 144

b. 1975 Merano, Italy

EDUCATION

1999 Goldschmiedeschule für Schmuck
und Gerät (Gold- and Silversmithing
School), Pforzheim, Germany
2003–06 BA Design, Faculty
of Design and Art, Free University
of Bozen, Italy (did not graduate)
2008–10 MA Product Design,
Royal College of Art, London, UK

PRACTICE

2010 Founded studio in Hackney,
London
2011 Interior Innovation Award, [D3]
Contest, IMM Cologne, Germany
2015 Founded studio in Lana, Italy
2016 Joined teaching staff of the
Faculty of Design and Art, Free
University of Bozen-Bolzano, Italy

Before turning to design, Thaler spent
several years training and working as a
goldsmith. A chance visit to a product-
design course while in Germany led
him to realize that his chosen medium,
jewelry, was too limited for his ideas. He
therefore returned to Italy and started
a BA in Design at his local university.
He completed the course but failed
the English exam, leaving him without
a graduation certificate. Undeterred,
he started an internship at the London
studio of the Italian designer Martino
Gamper and, two years later, was
accepted for a master's degree at the
Royal College of Art.

In 2011 Thaler exhibited the
Pressed chair – his final degree project
– at the IMM Cologne furniture fair. In
addition to receiving first prize in the
international newcomers competition,
he was noticed by the furniture
producer Nils Holger Moormann. Not
long afterwards the chair was added
to Moormann's collection and put into
production, helping to establish Thaler
as an innovative furniture designer.

Thaler occasionally collaborates with
Martino Gamper, most recently as part
of Gamper's 'From-To' project, which
brought together international designers
with local artisans in the Veneto district
of Italy. The results of the project were
presented at the 2015 Salone del Mobile
in Milan; Thaler's contribution consisted
of a chair made of sheet and tubular
steel, and lighting made of turned stone
and marble.

Michael Thonet p. 120

b. 1796 Boppard, Germany
d. 1871 Vienna, Austria

EDUCATION

c. 1810 Trained as a cabinetmaker
and carpenter in Boppard, Germany

PRACTICE

1819 Founded his own cabinetmaker's
workshop in Boppard
1830 Began experimenting with curved
laminated wood
1836–40 First-ever production of chairs
with laminated stretchers and backs
1841 Moved to Vienna; worked as a
cabinetmaker for Clemens List
1849 Founded his own workshop
in Vienna
1851 Showed his designs at the
Great Exhibition in London
1859 Production of the No. 14
steam-bent chair began

Michael Thonet embarked on his
furniture-making career in 1819; eleven
years later, he started experimenting with
laminated veneers, which allowed him to
form extreme curves and spirals for the
arms and legs of his chairs. When his first
venture in Germany went bankrupt, he
moved to Vienna, Austria, where he found
work as a cabinetmaker. It was also in
Vienna that he applied for and received
his first imperial patent, for the laminating
process he had developed. It would be
another eight years, however, before he
was financially independent enough to
set up his own workshop.

Thonet's first significant
commission, carried out in 1850,
was to furnish the immensely popular
Café Daum in Vienna with one of his
chairs, the No. 4 'Konsumsessel'. It was
the first café in the city to be supplied
with his laminated seating, and the
commission opened the way to large
commercial contracts. Building on this
success, Thonet established a new
company in 1853 with and for his sons:
Gebrüder Thonet (Thonet Brothers).
Shortly afterwards he was granted
a second patent, this time for his
new steam-bending process, which
would revolutionize the world of
furniture-making.

Despite the short period of
protection offered by this second
patent (thirteen years), Thonet's rational
designs and production methods
enabled him to dominate the market
for decades. Between 1859 and 1904
more than 45 million Thonet No. 14
chairs were sold worldwide. It is still in
production today.

Maarten Van Severen pp. 12, 104

b. 1956 Antwerp, Belgium
d. 2005 Ghent, Belgium

EDUCATION
Studied architecture at Sint-Lucas Ghent (course not completed)

PRACTICE
Early 1980s Worked in the office of the architect Monique Stoop; also started an interior architecture business with his brother Fabiaan
1986 Founded his own furniture workshop and started producing his first furniture designs
1990 Began collaboration with Rem Koolhaas
1994 Began collaboration with Vitra
1999 Ceased producing own furniture to focus on other projects

Van Severen, son of the abstract artist Dan Van Severen, worked for several years as an interior architect before founding his own workshop and producing his own furniture. His minimalist designs explore the concept of reduction, and often have an almost two-dimensional quality. Van Severen sometimes worked on a chair design for many years, searching for the best proportions and manufacturing techniques, before allowing it to be put into production. In 2008 the Maarten Van Severen Foundation was established by his widow, Marij de Brabandere, who is also a member of the foundation's board.

Marcel Wanders p. 92

b. 1963 Boxtel, the Netherlands

EDUCATION
1981–82 BA Industrial Design, Design Academy Eindhoven, the Netherlands (course not completed)
1982–83 Studied at the Academie voor Toegepaste Kunsten, Maastricht, the Netherlands
1983–85 Studied at the Academie voor Schone Kunsten, Hasselt, Belgium
1985–88 BA 3D Design, Hogeschool voor de Kunsten (now ArtEZ University of the Arts), Arnhem, the Netherlands

PRACTICE
1990–92 Worked for Landmark Design & Consult in Rotterdam
1990–93 Taught at the Hogeschool voor de Kunsten, Arnhem, the Gerrit Rietveld Academie, Amsterdam, and the Design Academy Eindhoven
1992–95 Partner in Waacs Design & Consultancy in Rotterdam
1995 Founded Wanders Wonders studio (later Marcel Wanders) in Amsterdam
2001 Co-founded design company Moooi
2014 Retrospective exhibition, 'Pinned Up', held at the Stedelijk Museum Amsterdam

After six years of studying design at three different universities, Wanders received his degree cum laude, confident that his unconventional approach – which had led to his expulsion from the then Bauhaus-focused Design Academy Eindhoven – was not without merit. Ultimately, Wanders would go on to co-found and direct one of Europe's largest design offices, Moooi, the success of which is based on anything but convention.

In 1993 Wanders took an important step on his journey towards international recognition by accepting an invitation to work with Droog, a newly founded collective of conceptual designers ('droog' being Dutch for 'dry', as in 'dry wit'). Through his association with Droog, Wanders took part in a number of experimental projects, including, in 1996, Dry Tech I – a collaboration with Delft University of Technology intended to explore the use of new materials. One of the outcomes of this project was Wanders's Knotted chair. Shown as part of Droog's 'Dry Tech I' exhibition at the 1996 Salone del Mobile in Milan, it attracted a great deal of attention, including that of its later producer, Cappellini.

Hans J. Wegner pp. 152, 216

b. 1914 Tønder, Denmark
d. 2007 Copenhagen, Denmark

EDUCATION
1928–32 Apprentice to master cabinetmaker H. F. Stahlberg, Tønder; obtained journeyman's certificate
1932–35 Military service in Copenhagen
1935 Cabinetmaking course, Teknologisk Institut, Copenhagen
1936–38 Studied furniture design at the School of Arts and Crafts, Copenhagen (course not completed)

PRACTICE
1938 Worked for the architects Erik Møller and Flemming Lassen, Aarhus, Denmark
1939–42 Worked for the architects Arne Jacobsen and Erik Møller, Aarhus
1943 Founded own studio in Aarhus
1946–53 Taught at School of Arts and Crafts, Copenhagen
1946–48 Worked for the architect Palle Suenson
1948 Returned to own studio in Aarhus

Wegner, whose father was a local shoemaker, was apprenticed to the master cabinetmaker H. F. Stahlberg at the age of fourteen. In his second year at the School of Arts and Crafts in Copenhagen, he was granted a year off to assist with the drawing of furniture for Arne Jacobsen and Erik Møller, who had just been awarded the commissions to design a new town hall in Aarhus and a public library in Nyborg. These two projects provided Wegner with so much experience and self-confidence that he did not return to college, deciding instead to continue working for the architects. After setting up his own office aged twenty-seven, Wegner would go on to become one of Denmark's most productive furniture designers.

Sori Yanagi p. 44

b. 1915 Tokyo, Japan
d. 2011 Tokyo, Japan

EDUCATION
1936–40 Studied painting and architecture at the School of Fine Arts (now University of the Arts), Tokyo
1947 Studied industrial design at the Industrial Arts Institute (IAI), Sendai, Japan

PRACTICE
1940–42 Worked as an assistant to Charlotte Perriand, Japan
1952 Awarded first prize at the inaugural New Japan Industrial Design Competition for a record player for Nippon Columbia
1952 Co-founded the Japanese Industrial Designers' Association, Tokyo
1952 Founded own office, Yanagi Institute for Industrial Design, Tokyo
1955–67 Professor of Industrial Design, Kanazawa College of Art, Japan
1957 Gold Medal for the Butterfly Stool at the Triennale di Milano, Italy
1964 Exhibited furniture at documenta 3, Kassel, Germany
1977 Appointed director of the Japan Folk Crafts Museum, Tokyo

When Yanagi's father, the philosopher and ceramics collector Soetsu Yanagi, founded the Japan Folk Crafts Museum in Tokyo in 1936, Sori was twenty-one years old and just about to start his architecture degree. Sori's background was thus strongly coloured by a love of the traditional craftsmanship found in everyday objects.

Yanagi's first contact with industrial design came when he worked as an assistant to the French designer Charlotte Perriand. Perriand had been invited to Japan to run the Industrial Arts Institute (IAI) in Sendai and, as an industrial-design consultant, to help Japan adjust to the opening up of world markets and its growing exports to the West. Perriand told her students about her work for Le Corbusier, about modernism, the standardization of forms and materials, using plywood and steel tubing in furniture design – all things that were relatively unknown in traditional Japanese folk crafts.

The two years he spent with Perriand made a profound impression on Yanagi, and his subsequent designs clearly include references to both worlds. Yanagi masterfully balanced the strengths of *mingei*, the Japanese folk art movement founded by his father, with the reduced functionalism and industrial production techniques of modernism.

Oskar Zieta p. 64

b. 1975 Zielona Góra, Poland

EDUCATION
1995 Graduated from Technical High School, Zielona Góra, with major in electronic engineering
2000 Completed architecture degree, Szczecin University of Technology, Poland
2000–01 Architectural studies as part of exchange programme, ETH Zurich, Switzerland
2001–03 Postgraduate scholarship in computer-aided architectural design (CAAD), ETH Zurich
2003–04 Research associate and teaching assistant, CAAD, Department of Architecture, ETH Zurich

PRACTICE
2007 Founded Zieta Prozessdesign in Zielona Góra
2007 Exhibited at the SaloneSatellite event, Salone del Mobile, Milan
2008 Plopp stool, the first furniture created using FiDU technology, put into production
2010 *Blow & Roll*, installation for London Design Festival, Victoria and Albert Museum, London
2017 Lecturer in industrial design at the School of Form in Poznań, Poland

Zieta's route into furniture design was indirect: after a sporting injury put paid to his intended athletics career, he turned to architecture. During his master's degree at ETH Zurich, Zieta joined a research team looking into ways of applying commercial metal-forming techniques to architectural constructions. Alongside bridge-like load-bearing structures, Zieta began to experiment with smaller objects using his newly developed FiDU (free inner-pressure deformation) process. In 200[?] ETH Zurich decided to sell off some of its old cutting and welding lasers; Zieta bought them and installed them in his father's factory, Steelwerk Polska, where he began preparing for production of the Plopp stool.

To launch his designs, Zieta applied for a stand at the 2007 Salone del Mobile in Milan, but it was fully booked. Luckily, however, two weeks before the start of the fair he was assigned a place following a cancellation. So, armed with prototypes of his furniture, 20,000 promotional leaflets and a caravan, he set off for Milan. The publicity and business contacts he gained there laid the foundations for his continuing success as an innovative designer.

Glossary

55MC

An example of the European Union reference used to denote a particular grade of steel. The number indicates the minimum yield stress, i.e. how much force the steel can withstand before deforming permanently, in this case 355 Newtons per square millimetre. The M stands for 'rolled thermo-mechanically', the C for 'special cold workability'. Steel with a minimum yield stress of 355 N/mm² and higher is termed 'high-tensile steel.' The EU standard is EN 10149-2.

ABS *see* **plastics**

brazing

A process by which two pieces of metal, the workpieces, are joined by the addition of molten metal used as a glue; not to be confused with *welding*. After the two workpieces – tubes, angles, plates, etc. – have been heated to more than 450°C, either with a blowtorch or a kiln, the brazing material (typically brass, tin or silver alloy) is introduced to the joint; a small amount melts and is drawn into the gap between the parts (ideally 0.05mm in width) by capillary action. At the stated temperature, the brazing material forms a metallurgical bond with the workpieces, creating a bond that is as strong as the alloy being used. It is extremely important that the surfaces of the workpieces are cleaned in advance, and coated with a *flux* to prevent oxidation during the heating. Unlike *welding* or *soldering*, brazing cannot be used to fill gaps; on the contrary, the larger the gap between the workpieces, the weaker the joint. Also, as opposed to *welding*, the bond can be reversed by heating the filler to melting temperature and lifting the pieces apart. As brazing is performed well below the melting point of the workpieces, there is little danger of thermal distortion or affecting the metallurgy. Brazing can be performed on steel, brass, copper, bronze, cast iron and aluminium, using the appropriate brazing alloys. *Soldering* is similar to brazing, but uses much lower temperatures; neither should it be confused with silver-soldering, silver-brazing or hard-soldering, all of which involve brazing using a silver alloy.

BSW

British Standard Whitworth, the very first national screw-thread standard, introduced in Britain in 1841 by Sir Joseph Whitworth. It specifies a standard thread angle of 55°. The thread pitch (the gap between the threads) varies with the screw size, according to a table devised by Whitworth. The standard is still in use today.

cane

A natural material, also known as rattan, used in seating. Strips of cane, made from the skin of the rattan vine, woven together to form a seating surface. Grown in Indonesia, the Philippines and Malaysia, the vine can reach lengths of up to 300 metres. The skin is shiny and relatively water-resistant. Once the skin has been removed from the vine, the thicker stems can be used to make the frame and legs of a chair, which are then covered or bound up in cane.

captive nut *see* **threaded insert**

casting

Usually, casting refers to a hot forming process. Starting with the material in an amorphous liquid state, the temperature is lowered, causing the material to solidify and take on the shape of the (heat-resistant) mould or form. The simplest example is making ice cubes: a one-part mould, usually with sloping sides (the *draft angle*) to ease the removal of the cast cube, is filled with liquid water and cooled. The same process can be used for almost any thermoplastic material, e.g. metals, plastics and glass. There are many variations on the process, determined by different melting points and thus starting temperatures, different mould materials and the force with which the material is introduced into the mould. The mould itself can be very simple – a depression pressed into a box of sand, filled by pouring (*sand-casting*) – or complex, such as a hollow steel block, divided into two or more interlocking parts, and filled under pressure through a nozzle (*high-pressure casting*). The choice of casting process will be influenced by such factors as the required definition and detail of the cast object, the intended surface treatment, budget and size of production run.

chrome

This shiny, non-corroding metal (chemical symbol Cr) is used almost exclusively as a very thin protective or decorative coating on other metals, i.e. chrome plating, never as a solid metal in its own right. Steel, iron, copper and brass can be chrome-plated directly; aluminium and plastic need an intermediate layer of another metal, such as nickel. Chrome is also the principal material added to steel to form stainless steel, with alloys containing around 12% for standard applications and up to 26% for highly corrosive situations, e.g. marine environments.

CSK

Abbreviation of the term 'countersunk' or 'countersink'. Refers either to a screw with an inverse conical head, or to the hole prepared to accept such a screw. The angle of the conical section, also known as the chamfer angle, can vary; the most common is 82°, followed by 90°. The countersinking tool and the countersunk screws being used must have the same chamfer angle.

draft angle

The angle of slope given to the walls of a mould used in *casting* or *injection moulding* to facilitate the removal of the workpiece after casting. If the walls of a moulding are vertical, the friction between them and the mould can prevent the workpiece from being taken out. If the walls are sloped outwards, i.e. given a draft angle, the piece can be more easily removed. Different materials require different draft angles; it usually lies between 1.5 and 3°, but can be as high as 5°.

flanging

A process applied to sheet metal, sometimes known as rolling, which mechanically turns over or bends the edge of the sheet, or hole. The desired result is a stiffening of the sheet, or a softening of the sharp edge. Flanging can be performed using a machine press, dies or a hand tool. A good example of the use of flanging can be seen on the Landi chair (p. 96).

flux

A material used to prevent metal surfaces oxidizing during *soldering*, *brazing* or *welding*. Oxidation is to be avoided, as it creates a surface layer of metal oxide, which prevents a good bond with the molten filling metal during the joining process. Flux materials are usually complex chemical compounds, sometimes poisonous and corrosive, so great care must be taken when using them. They can be in liquid form, and thus painted on to the workpieces, or hard, e.g. pre-baked on to a welding electrode. Oxidation can also be avoided by heating the workpieces in a vacuum chamber, or by shrouding them in a flow of inert gas (argon, helium or carbon dioxide) during the joining process.

GRP *see* **plastics**

high-pressure casting

This casting process involves molten metal being forced into a mould at a very high pressure. In the case of aluminium, for example, two or more hardened steel moulds or dies are pre-warmed to around 500°C and then filled with 1,220°C molten aluminium using a pressure of 100–1,000 bar. The benefits are greater levels of detail and thinner wall thicknesses than can be achieved using *low-pressure casting*; the drawbacks are the high costs of the hardened dies. High-pressure casting can be used for a variety of metals, including zinc and magnesium alloys, brass, copper, lead, tin and bronze. When plastic is moulded using this process, it is known as *injection moulding*.

injection moulding

Essentially the same process as *high-pressure casting*, but using plastic instead of metal. A hot, molten material is forced under pressure into a mould in which it then cools down and solidifies, taking on the form of the mould. Usually, the material is a plastic such as *PP*, *PS* or *ABS*. The mould is commonly made of hardened steel, and is cooled by water flowing through internal channels to speed up the cycle, i.e. injection of hot material, cooling phase, ejection of the finished object. The mould is necessarily closed to the outside atmosphere, being made up of two or more parts that form a seal with each other. More complex moulds can have moving parts, which shift after the first injection, creating a space next to the moulding and allowing a second injection using a different colour or consistency of plastic. An example of the use of this technique is the addition of soft 'grip-strips' on the handles of tools.

kerf

A slot cut into the top edge of a *tenon* to allow a wedge to be hammered in, tightening up the *mortice* and *tenon* joint. Wider tenons can have two or more kerfs. The wedges are visible from the outside of the joint (see the Pelt chair, p. 140), which means they can be used as decorative constructional details.

laser-cutting

This process uses a laser to cut out shapes in sheet material, e.g. paper, cardboard, metal and plastic. The sheet is positioned and held stationary on a flat surface; the laser is mounted on a movable arm a few centimetres above the sheet, pointing downwards. The laser is then moved over the sheet by a CNC (computer numerical control) program, cutting the material as it goes. In the case of thin sheet materials, a high-performance laser can move at speeds faster than the eye can follow. By controlling its power, the laser can also be used to weld sheets, with some laser-cutting machines able to perform cutting and welding on the same workpiece. The process is not limited to 2D sheets; some lasers are designed to move in six axes, enabling them to cut intricately shaped into a 3D form (see the Veryround chair, p. 204).

LDPE *see* **plastics**

lost-foam casting

A variation of *sand-casting*. Instead of impressing then removing the usual wooden pattern (design model) from the mould, a pattern made of polystyrene foam is put into the mould and covered in the casting sand. The pattern has extra rods (known as sprues) fixed to its edges, which lead upwards through the sand and form the entry channels for the casting metal. When the molten metal is poured into the mould, the foam pattern burns away instantly, allowing the metal to take its place in the resulting space. After lifting the hardened casting from the sand, the sprues and any uneven residues are cut off in a process known as *trimming*.

lost-wax casting

This process is similar to *lost-foam casting*, but is much older, having been used by the Assyrians in 200 BC. A wax pattern (design model) is made and embedded in a ceramic material. The latter is then dried and heated, causing the wax to melt and run out. Moulten metal is poured into the resulting mould, which, when it is cool enough, is broken open to retrieve the casting.

low-pressure casting

A process similar to *high-pressure casting*. A mould made of cast iron or steel (usually in two parts) is positioned on top of an air-tight chamber containing a heated crucible of molten aluminium; a tube from the bottom of the mould reaches down into the liquid metal. Air is pumped into the crucible chamber at a pressure of approximately 1 bar, forcing the molten metal up the tube and filling the mould above. The advantage of this process is greater precision and detailing compared to sand-casting. In addition, the pressure from the crucible causes the mould to fill continuously, preventing hollows in the surfaces of the casting, which shrinks slightly as it cools down.

MDF

Middle-density fibreboard. A sheet material, commonly employed in furniture and interior projects, made of very fine wood fibres, compressed and bonded using an urea-formaldehyde resin. Its density lies between 600 and 800kg/m³ (HDF, high-density fibreboard, has a density of 800–1,000kg/m³). Although the fibres are fine and randomly distributed, some panels tend to bend more easily over their length than their width. It is also worth noting that the surface layer is denser than the inner zone, which plays a part when the cut edge is visible. The typical sheet size is 122 x 240cm, with thicknesses ranging from 3–50mm; surface colours include black and various muted tones, as well as its natural brown state. It is also available in a flexible form, in which one side of the sheet has been slotted with a regular pattern of deep cuts, allowing the sheet to be curved before fixing.

metric thread

A system for denoting the size of general-purpose machine screws, shortened to M, e.g. M6, where 6 is the diameter in millimetres of the threaded part of the screw. While it is used principally to describe the screw thread, the system can also refer to the size of the threaded screw hole, e.g. tapped M6. For every screw size, there are two related drill sizes: a clearance size, which results in a hole large enough for the screw to pass through unheeded, and a tapping size, which creates a hole that, once threaded, the screw can be screwed into. An M6 screw, for example, requires a clearance drill of Ø6.6mm and a tapping drill of Ø5mm. There are extensive tables for clearance and tapping sizes for all metric threads. It is worth noting that metric-thread screws are also available in fine pitch, i.e. with more threads per centimetre. For instance, an M6 is available in 0.5mm fine and 0.75mm fine, as well as 1.0mm standard pitch. However, fine pitch screws are very rarely used in furniture construction. See also *screw threads*.

mortice *see* **tenon**

multiplex *see* **plywood**

nylon-insert lock nut
A self-securing nut, which cannot be shaken or vibrated off its bolt; used as an alternative to a *threadlocker*. The nut incorporates a ring of nylon with a slightly smaller diameter at the outside end of the thread. When the nut is screwed on to its bolt, the bolt end has to be forced passed this ring, creating enough friction to hold the nut in place.

plastics
There is a huge variety of plastic materials on the market. Below is a list of the more common families of compounds, together with their main characteristics:

ABS Acrylonitrile butadiene styrene. A high-quality, hard, strong plastic, with which a moulding with a high-gloss surface can be realized; applications include furniture and household goods. Used in the first version of the Universale chair (p. 200); later changed to nylon then *PP*.

GRP Glass-filled reinforced plastic. Woven mats of fibreglass are laid in a mould and soaked in a two-part epoxy resin. Used extensively in the 1950s and 1960s for furniture and boat-building, but its manufacture is labour-intensive. See the PAW chair (p. 136).

PA Polyamides. A group of plastics that includes such materials as nylon and Kevlar. Can be very strong, with good abrasive resistance; it is also self-lubricating. See the Universale chair (p. 200).

PE Polyethylene. A very common plastic, strong, flexible and resilient. Available in various densities up to ultra-high-density (UHDPE), sold as Dyneema, which is 40% stronger than Kevlar. In its linear low-density version (LLDPE), it is used in *rotational moulding*. See the Orgone Plastic chair (p. 124).

PP Polypropylene. A widely used plastic with very high fatigue resistance. It cannot be glued (hence its use for the tops of tubes of adhesive) but is easily welded. Very flexible, so ideal for hinges and clips; also used in *rotational moulding* and for chair shells. Can be reinforced by adding finely chopped glass strands. See the Air and DSW chairs (pp. 20 and 80 respectively).

PS Polystyrene. In solid form, relatively cheap but brittle. Used for the first injection-moulded Panton chair (p. 132). In its expanded form, used as packaging, especially in blocks or chips.

PU Polyurethane, also known as polyurethane resin (PUR). Available in a wide variety of forms, including hard and soft foams, as well as in blocks and sheets; can also be used for *injection moulding*. See the .03 chair (p. 12) for its use as a self-skinning foam.

PVC Polyvinyl chloride. Used as a textile or membrane; also available in a rigid form (uPVC). Releases poisonous chlorine and dioxins when burnt, so no longer acceptable in many situations. See the Blow chair (p. 40).

TPE Thermoplastic elastomers. A family of plastics that combine the qualities of a plastic with those of an elastomer, i.e. they can be injection-moulded but are very elastic, rubbery and resilient. Used extensively in the automobile and electronics industries. In furniture design, their flexibility and abrasive resistance mean they are often used for feet and stoppers. See the Landi chair (p. 96).

plywood
A man-made wooden board material consisting of at least three layers, or plies, of wood veneer bonded together with wood glue or resin. The number of layers is usually odd, with the plies built up symmetrically around a central layer. The grain direction is alternated by 90° with each layer, a process that helps prevent distortion or warping. An exception to this is bendable or flexible plywood, in which all the layers are facing the same way. This results in a sheet that can be flexed in one direction. The outward-facing plies are usually a hardwood (e.g. beech, maple or oak) between 0.5 and 1mm thick, while the inner plies are often a cheaper conifer softwood of thicker dimensions. Multiplex is a high-quality version of plywood in which all the layers are of the same thickness and material, bonded together using waterproof glue; it is also stiffer, heavier and more expensive than standard plywood. There are various grades of water-resistance for different situations, from humid rooms up to a marine environment. The layers in Multiplex are between 0.8 and 2.5mm thick, with standard board thicknesses ranging from 6.5 to 40mm. The choice of wood includes beech, birch, maple and meranti.

powder coating
A finishing process, usually applied to metal, that produces a very durable and effective coating. First, using a technique known as electrostatic spray deposition (ESD), a dry polymer resin powder is sprayed on to the workpiece, which has been electrically grounded, using a spray gun that gives the powder an electrostatic charge; this causes the powder to be evenly attracted to the surface of the workpiece. In a second stage, the workpiece is baked in a curing oven, in which the resin not only melts to produce a uniform finish, but also forms long molecular chains, thus increasing the durability of the coating. Through the use of additives, the glossiness, texture and thickness of the coating

can be adjusted as required. Standard curing takes place at 160–200°C; by also using ultraviolet light, the temperature can be reduced to 80–140°C, thereby allowing a wider range of materials, including *MDF* and *plastics*, to be powder-coated. Such materials, however, often have to be treated with a conductive coating beforehand.

PVD *see* **sputtering**

rails
There are two kinds of rails: those that make up the backrest, called top, middle and lower rails; and those that make up the *seating frame*, called front, side and rear rails, all of which run horizontally between the legs. Front and side rails usually meet at the top of the front leg. Seating-frame rails are sometimes misleadingly called *stretchers*; the front rail is also sometimes termed an apron.

rattan *see* **cane**

rotational moulding
A process for casting large hollow plastic forms without using either a core in the mould or pressure to inject the plastic. Items produced using this process include boats, liquid containers and furniture. A two- or multipart mould, made of aluminium or sheet steel, is mounted on gimbals, enabling it to be rotated and turned in all directions. The mould is loaded with a measured amount of plastic granulate, e.g. LLDPE (see *PE*). It is then brought up to temperature while being kept in motion, causing the plastic to melt and flow over the inside surface of the mould. The rotation is continued while cooling to prevent the moulded form from sagging. Once the plastic has cooled sufficiently, the mould is opened and the workpiece removed. Usually, certain cutting or drilling operations are then carried out to open up parts of the workpiece (e.g. the Orgone Plastic chair, p. 124) or to fit fastenings.

sand-casting
Used for casting metal or glass. The mould is built up or formed by pressing a wooden pattern (design model) into a box of casting sand. Often, the top and bottom or two sides of a pattern will be formed in two separate boxes, which are then clamped together to allow the whole part to be cast in one go. The pattern includes a number of sprues (see *lost-foam casting*), which are cut off after moulding. Casting sand is a mixture of silica sand (89%), clay (7%) and water (4%). Sometimes, additional chemicals are added to the sand to alter its properties, depending on the complexity of the pattern and the metal being cast. The more accurate the pattern, the better the casting. In the early 20th century, before the profession of model-maker was established, industrial designers used pattern-makers to make their design models. The advantages of sand casting are that the process is relatively cheap, and both the pattern and the sand can be reused. The disadvantages are the relatively thick walls, rough surfaces and low overall accuracy of the resulting

workpiece, as compared to using more expensive metal moulds.

scarf joint
A method of joining two pieces of wood end to end. To increase the adhesive surface, the two pieces are cut at a sloping angle, usually in the region of 8–10°. The smaller the angle, the longer the joint will be. An example of a 4° scarf joint can be seen in the side frames of the Paimio chair (p. 128).

screw threads
The thread of machine screws and bolts is defined by the width of the threaded portion, the thread angle (the angle of the flanks) and the pitch (the distance between the threads). The angle at which the thread rises, i.e. the slope in relation to the work surface, is termed the helic angle. The number that appears in the usual terminology for screws – e.g. M3, BSF ⁵⁄₁₆ – refers to the diameter (in millimetres or, in the case of pre-metric standards, fractions of an inch) of the threaded section. Historically, many companies developed their own threads for specific purposes. In the 19th century, for example, the Birmingham Small Arms Company developed its BSA threads, which are still the standard thread sizes for the bottom brackets of bicycles. The BSW (British Standard Whitworth) was the very first national standard, used for such larger construction projects as shipbuilding. Established in 1841, it is still used today in piping and hydraulic work. The BSF (British Standard Fine) was developed for smaller engineering work, and has the same thread angle (55°) as BSW threads but a narrower pitch. Over the years, the metric system (with a 60° thread angle) has become the standard for European chairs. Metric threads are available in both standard and fine versions. See also *metric thread*.

seating frame
The part of a chair construction that provides a basis for the seating surface. Usually made of four elements, and forming a rectangle or trapezium, it has a double function: to join the top of the front legs to the rear legs, and to support the seat. The individual parts of the frame are known as *rails* (front, side, rear), but are sometimes misleadingly called *stretchers*.

slot hole
A rectangular hole with the ends extended to form half-circles, as though a tool has first of all drilled a round hole before being moved sideways to elongate the hole. Also known as an elongated or slotted hole.

soldering
This process, also known as soft-soldering, is similar in nature to *brazing*. However, the joining materials used (solders) are lead- or silver-based alloys, which melt at relatively low temperatures, i.e. below 350°C, and even as low as 180°C. At these temperatures no metallurgical bonding takes place, so the joints are much weaker. Soldering is commonly used in the electronics industry, for joining

components together. Designers often use it in model-making; for full-size prototyping and furniture production, the bond formed is too weak to be viable. Soldering is not to be confused with silver-soldering, silver-brazing or hard-soldering, all of which are forms of *brazing* using a silver alloy.

spot-welding
A quick and simple way of joining pieces of sheet metal together; also known as resistance spot welding (RSW). Two metal electrodes, fixed at the ends of opposing arms like giant fingers, are brought together, clamping the workpieces (e.g. two sheets of metal) between their tips. At that moment, a pulse of high-current, low-voltage electricity (e.g. 1.5V, 5,000A, for 0.5 seconds) flows between the electrodes, generating sufficient heat through electrical resistance to melt the two small areas (spots) of metal between the tips. The mechanical pressure applied by the electrodes causes these spots to fuse together, forming a join. The size of the spots varies between Ø3mm and Ø13mm, depending on the required strength of the join and the thickness of the materials being welded. The spots are often set in a row around the edge of a workpiece. In the car industry, robots can set the spots every second or so. When performed in a workshop, it is a much gentler process: the operator holds the workpieces in his hands, introduces the place to be welded between the electrodes, and activates the machine with a foot pedal. The electrode arms close; there is a brief humming noise; sometimes a small spark; the arms open again; and the piece is welded.

sputtering
A method of coating a surface with a thin film of another material; also known as physical vapour deposition (PVD). It can be used to coat a metal with a protective layer of another non-corroding metal or compound, e.g. coating aluminium with titanium, or to give stainless steel a coloured surface of nitrides or carbides. A piece of the chosen coating material (e.g. titanium) is bombarded with very high-energy gas ions, dislodging atoms of the coating material from its surface. These atoms hit the workpiece with great energy, bonding with and partly penetrating the surface, and slowly accumulating to form a very durable coating. The process is capable of transferring metals with very high melting points, producing resilient and corrosion-free surface finishes previously unattainable. Originally used in the semi-conductor and jewelry industries, it has only recently been introduced into other fields. One disadvantage of the process is that the workpieces have to be placed inside a vacuum chamber, thus limiting the size of the parts to be treated. Chair-sized objects, however, are within the limitations; see Chair One (p. 56).

stile
The part of a chair construction that supports the backrest; also known as